T0109500

Thoughtful Wisdom
for Every Day

Thoughtful Wisdom for Every Day

365 Days of Love, Kindness, Healing, Faith, and Peace

Leo Tolstoy

Selected and Translated from the Russian by Peter Sekirin

Arcade Publishing • New York

English-language translation, introduction, and compilation
copyright © 2005 by Peter Sekirin

First Arcade/Skyhorse Hardcover Edition 2021

Arcade Publishing books may be purchased in bulk at special
discounts for sales promotion, corporate gifts, fund-raising, or
educational purposes. Special editions can also be created to
specifications. For details, contact the Special Sales Department,
Arcade Publishing, 307 West 36th Street, 11th Floor, New
York, NY 10018 or arcade@skyhorsepublishing.com.

Arcade Publishing® is a registered trademark of Skyhorse
Publishing, Inc.®, a Delaware corporation.

Visit our website at www.arcadepub.com.

10 9 8 7 6 5 4 3 2 1

Library of Congress Cataloging-in-Publication Data is available
on file.

Cover design by Erin Seaward-Hiatt
Cover illustration: Ceneri/Getty Images

ISBN: 978-1-951627-89-8
Ebook ISBN: 978-1-950994-39-7

Printed in the United States of America

ACKNOWLEDGMENTS

I would like to express my sincere acknowledgments to the following people: my friends Karla Lees, Kim Yates, Phil Hill, and Patrick Parnaby for their help with the initial editing of the manuscript and selection of the wise thoughts; my editor, Cal Barksdale, for his professional advice, expertise, and wisdom; and my wife, Helen, parents, Vera and Vsevolod, and children, Matthew, Marina, George, and Elias for all their inspiration and support.

INTRODUCTION
Tolstoy's Last Major Work: Its Importance, the History of Its Creation and Publication, and Its Major Message

The Thoughts of Wise Men was Leo Tolstoy's final work, the one he loved more than all others and considered his most important single contribution to humanity. In it, Tolstoy distilled and presented the spiritual wisdom of many nations, cultures, and historical periods to create an original work, unsurpassed by anything in world literature. As his source, he drew from the world's sacred texts, major religions, and great philosophical systems and the literary works of more than three hundred of his favorite authors.

Tolstoy devoted the last eight years of his life to this project, which took shape as a trilogy of books that evolved over several editions:

The Thoughts of Wise Men (1903);
A Circle of Reading (1906), first published in English in 1997 by Scribner under the title *A Calendar of Wisdom*;
Thoughtful Wisdom for Every Day (1909), recently rediscovered in Russia and now published in English for the first time.

The Thoughts of Wise Men (1903)

The first book contained only one to three thoughts per day, about eight hundred in all, with forty-one authors represented. It was relatively short, and the thoughts were arranged randomly and not thematically linked: they were just a collection of intellectual gems by Tolstoy's favorite writers. The booklet enjoyed considerable success and went through more than a dozen editions, one every year starting in 1903. It was even published as a desktop gift calendar. Its popularity led Tolstoy to revisit and rethink this project in 1904, with a view to creating a book that would be "necessary for everyone," and he spent most of his time and literary energy on it.

A Circle of Reading (1906)

Tolstoy at first set to work revising and enlarging *The Thoughts of Wise Men*. At the beginning of 1904, he wrote in his diary, "I am busy improving *The Thoughts*." Several months later, though, it became obvious that he was not merely editing: he was working on the creation of a completely new book, different from *The Thoughts* in its structure, size, volume, and quality. At the outset, Tolstoy referred to this new project as *A New Calendar*, or sometimes *A Calendar of Wisdom*, but he soon began to call it *A Circle of Reading*.

He first mentioned it by this title in his letter to G. Rusanov on September 24, 1904: "During the last days I have been busy: I'm not working on my *Calendar* anymore but on *A Circle of Reading* every day."

The thoughts in this new book were organized around daily topics such as love, God, friendship, life, and children, spread throughout the twelve months. The work moved slowly owing to the huge amount of source material. Tolstoy read and reread more than three hundred books while he worked on the second part of the trilogy, and the *Calendar* grew from three dozen pages to many hundreds. Each entry included five to seven, sometimes more, wise thoughts—over two thousand in total—carefully selected from Tolstoy's library of more than 22,000 volumes, from the works of over 250 of the greatest thinkers and writers of all time, and, in the case of several hundred thoughts, from fifty different collections of quotations in Russian, French, English, and German.

Every day started and ended with a thought by Tolstoy himself, styled in italics. The writer also added fifty-two weekly readings, which consisted of a short story or a chapter from a novel by one of his favorite writers, among them Anton Chekhov, Fyodor

Dostoyevsky, Gustave Flaubert, Victor Hugo, and Plato. The book became so large that it was published not as a single volume but as twelve monthly booklets in 1906. It went through numerous editions between 1907 and 1915.

However, this second work of his trilogy lacked to a certain degree coherence and integrity. There was no general structure or message for the whole book, the topics repeated more or less randomly and were not linked to a specific day of the month, the days lacked headings, and even the weekly readings were inconsistent, varying between fiction and nonfiction.

Thoughtful Wisdom for Every Day
(1909)

From 1906 to 1909, Tolstoy became so preoccupied with this project that he decided to produce another, similar book, to be titled *The Thoughts of Wise Men for Every Day*. The title was eventually shortened to *For Every Day*. With this work, the writer fully achieved what he intended: *For Every Day* had a definite structure, with a monthly cycle of repeating themes, and it was more focused, more precise, and at the same time more accessible to a broad readership.

Each day of the year consisted of nine to twelve aphorisms or thoughts. In the previous book, Tolstoy had added another two hundred authors to those cited in the first. However, this time the bulk of the book was comprised of wise thoughts written by Tolstoy himself. Then, Tolstoy came up with an unusual, breakthrough idea: he created thirty topics (God, love, faith, soul, truth, and so forth) to correspond to each day of the month, and, with some variation, repeated the same structure every month. Tolstoy stressed in correspondence to his friend, the literary critic, V. Posse, that this book was different from anything he had ever written because of the scope and type of material.

Tolstoy's last great project seems to have grown out of his close brush with death late in life. In the spring of 1902, when he was seventy-five, Tolstoy fell seriously ill, first with pneumonia and then with typhoid fever. No antibiotics had been invented at that time, and both diseases were considered potentially fatal. Tolstoy hung precariously between life and death for several months. His survival was little short of miraculous. While he was recuperating in November–December 1902 in the small town of Gaspra, near Yalta in Crimea, he was unable to work in his usual way, so he often met with fellow writers Chekhov, Gorky, and others, and talked about life, death, literature, and the meaning of life. He got into the habit of reading and reflecting on a single nugget of wisdom each day, taken from a wall calendar that hung in his room. The calendar ended on December 1902.

The next month, in January 1903, confronted with the lack of a ready-made subject of meditation, Tolstoy realized that he had developed a useful and rewarding habit. When he had entirely recovered from his illness, he began collecting the thoughts of wise men from his own library for his personal pleasure.

Thus did he gradually embark on a project that would take up almost all of the last eight years of his life, that is, from 1903 to 1910, and would become a trilogy of more than 1,200 pages in length. This work would summarize the writer's views on life and God, and he would refer to it as "much more important" than anything he had ever written before. The first idea for this book had actually appeared much earlier, about twenty years before his illness, when Tolstoy wrote in his diary on March 15, 1884: "It would be nice to make a circle of reading: Epictetis, Marcus Aurelius, Buddha, Pascal, and the New Testament. And it is necessary for everyone." A year later, he repeated the same thought in a letter to his assistant Chertkov dated June 4–5, 1885: "I would like to compile a circle of reading, that is, excerpts from the books that tell us about what a man needs most in his life, and what is good for him." Although his other literary projects preempted this work, he returned to the idea in 1903, after his illnesses and recovery.

Finally, a few remarks about the present publication and continued relevance of *Thoughtful Wisdom for Every Day*. Tolstoy's trilogy was immensely popular from the publication of the first volume in 1903 until the revolution in 1917. Then all three volumes were banned by the Soviet regime for almost eighty years because of their religious content. Rediscovered after the fall of the Soviet Union, they have enjoyed a tremendous success in Russia in recent years, with over three editions and 300,000 copies in print. *Thoughtful Wisdom for Every Day* is the last of the volumes to be rediscovered, and it is being translated into English and published here for the first time.

This book, Tolstoy's last great work, is as important now, nearly a hundred years after its creation, as it was when it was first published. The depth of Tolstoy's wisdom, his faith, and his intelligence shine through clearly. His thoughts are the distillation of the best of several thousand years of human experience, and they are as fresh, genuine, and applicable now as they ever were. Tolstoy teaches his readers to ponder, to wonder, to laugh, and most of all, to understand the human condition with clarity and deep sympathy. This is a classic—and timeless—*Chicken Soup for Your Soul*.

The structure of *Thoughtful Wisdom for Every Day* is elaborate but also flexible. Each month is divided into four sections—Our Relationship with God, Our Challenges, Our Actions, and Our Spiritual Life—that cover a variety of themes, one for each day. For example, Our Relationship with God begins the month and comprises the themes of faith, soul, one soul in all, God, unification in spirit, and universal love. The next group, Our Challenges, introduces the themes of our sins and temptations, inequality, false science, judgment and punishment, and violence and war. Our Actions is dedicated to the themes of spiritual effort and virtue, thoughts, words and actions, truth and lies, humility, self-sacrifice, prayer, and work. The last section, Our Spiritual Life, includes the themes of living in the present, evil and suffering, death, life after death, happiness, and love. The themes recur from month to month according to this cycle, but the days may vary somewhat and a theme may repeat or be absent in a given month.

For this edition, which is selective, I have chosen the thoughts that seemed the most original and suitable for our time and that were not redundant. In this sort of collection, where Tolstoy considered thoughts from diverse angles, there is inevitably some repetition.

Tolstoy kept his guide to living a good life on his desk during his final years until the very end (he even asked his assistant, V. Chertkov, to bring him the galleys on his deathbed). He made a habit of reading from it to his family and recommended it highly to his friends. Now, in a time of growing spiritual awareness, Tolstoy's great self-help masterpiece is once again available to provide readers everywhere with inspiration and solace and, as he wished, to "help them in their life and work."

Introduction by Leo Tolstoy to
For Every Day

This book, *The Thoughts of Wise Men for Every Day*, is written in the same manner as, and is similar in structure, to my previous book, *A Circle of Reading* [*A Calendar of Wisdom* in the English translation]. It consists of a collection of thoughts for each day of the year.

The major difference between this and the previous book is that the new thoughts in this volume are arranged, not at random, as was the case in the previous book, but according to a logical system. From one month to the next, the daily thoughts follow a particular sequence, each one being meaningful in relation to those that preceded it. Thereby, the days are interconnected. Also, each and every month comprises a particular philosophical outlook that can be used to guide our actions. This outlook is illustrated with the thoughts of ancient and present-day thinkers from different nations.

The names of the thinkers—from whom I have borrowed thoughts—are given here. However, many of the thoughts were changed and/or shortened, thus reflecting the ways in which I understood them. The thoughts that are unattributed were written by me.

I hope the readers of this book will experience the same benevolent and uplifting feeling that I experienced while working on its creation and that I continue to feel again and again when I reread it every day.

1908–1910

Faith

 The law of God involves fulfilling God's will. Because all people are created equal, the law of God is the same for all of us. Our lives can be good only when we understand the law of God and follow it.

According to an old Jewish saying, "A person's soul is God's lamp." A person is helpless when God's lamp is not lit, but becomes strong and free when it is. Of course, this cannot be otherwise, because it is not their own power but God's.

Although we don't know what universal goodness is, we do know that we should all follow the law of goodness that exists in both human wisdom and our hearts.

If people believe that they can please God through rituals and prayers alone — not by deeds — then they have lied to both God and themselves.

1

Soul

What do I call my "inner self"? It is my soul, which lives in and is connected to my body. We all pass through particular stages as we age. First, we are infants, then children, then men or women, and finally we grow old. But during this time, our inner self remains the same. This inner self is our soul.

Understanding ourselves involves realizing that life is not within the body but within the soul.

Iron is stronger than stone, stone is stronger than wood, wood is stronger than water, and water is stronger than air. But there is something that we can neither feel, nor see, nor hear that is stronger than anything else. It existed before, it exists now, it will always exist and will never disappear. What is it? It is spirit, the soul that lives in every person.

We are amazed at the size of a big mountain, the sun, or the stars in the universe. But these great things are nothing compared to our souls — the most powerful thing in the world.

One Soul in All

 A river does not look like a pond, nor a pond like a barrel, and a barrel looks different from a glass of water. But each holds the same water within. Likewise, it is the same spirit that lives in all kinds of people — a healthy adult, a sick child, a young king, or a poor woman. The same spirit gives life to us all.

When we see in others the same spirit that lives in us, we feel as if we have awakened from a long sleep.

We are united with all people and all creatures. Thus, we must treat as we would like to be treated not only other people but animals as well.

God lives in every kind person.

If people could understand that they do not live individual lives but that their lives and souls are linked to others', then they would know that in doing good deeds for others, they do good for themselves.

God

 People often say that God is love, or that love is God. People also say that God is intellect, or that the intellect partakes of God's power. But this cannot be the case. Love and the intellect are qualities of God that are known to us. What God is we certainly do not know.

Everyone can feel God, but no one can truly understand God. Thus, do not attempt to understand God, but try instead to feel God's presence within you. If you are unable to find God there, then you will never find Him.

When you look inside yourself, you see what is called "your own self" or your soul. You cannot touch it or see it or understand it, but you know it is there. And this part of yourself — that which you cannot understand — is what is called God. God is both around us and inside of us — in our souls.

The more you understand that you are at one with God, the more you will understand that you are at one with all His worldly manifestations.

Unification in Spirit

When Socrates was asked where he was born, he answered, "On this earth." When he was asked of which state he was a citizen, he answered, "A citizen of the world." We must remember those profound words. We all live on the same earth, under God's great power, which is superior to that of men, and under God's law.

We know in our hearts that we should strive for unification with all people. The more united we become, the better our lives will be. Likewise, the more we separate from each other, the worse our lives will be.

Every person has two masters: the body and the soul. When the body rules, one struggles and experiences animosity toward others. However, the more one grows in spiritual understanding, the more one's internal power transfers to the soul — to the spirit that seeks unification with the souls of others.

Universal Love

Every person loves his or her own self, and there is absolutely nothing wrong with this. However, to love only the body is to bring suffering to others.

You become what you love. If you love earthly things, you will become earth. If you love God, then you will become part of God.

Love that is caused by something else, that has a reason, is not pure love. Only love without limits — unconditional love — is eternal. It does not disappear but grows continuously with time.

There can be neither virtue nor goodness without love.

Pride

 People tend to be proud of things for which they should be ashamed, such as their wealth or power over others.

A person can believe that he or she is better than someone else only when the other's character is not truly known.

When you perform acts of goodness, it is often difficult to tell for certain whether you do them for the soul, for God, for another person, or to satisfy your own pride. It is easy to tell, though, if you ask yourself whether you would do these things if no one was made aware of them. When you perform acts of goodness anonymously, you do so for your soul and for God.

It is all right when people praise you for your work. But it is wrong to do your work in order to be praised by others.

Vanity and Fame

You cannot be loved and praised by all. Indeed, if you act as a good person, bad people will scold you. If you act as a bad person, good people will disapprove of your actions. The best solution is to be kind and good while ignoring the opinions of others.

Only those who have abandoned their soul for fame and wealth will be concerned about the opinions of others.

Nourish your soul, not your fame or popularity.

If a person is free from vanity, it is easier to serve God.

One who lives a true life does not need praise or fame.

Greed and Wealth

 A person who lives among the needy but is wealthy and proud of that wealth lives a life in the absence of truth.

People who spend all their lives acquiring wealth will never be satisfied. The wealthier they become, the more they want, and so on without end.

You must remember that life is a lesson. This lesson is about how to nourish your soul, and those who, instead of nourishing their soul, dedicate their lives to acquiring wealth are mistaken.

It is obvious that the rich see their wealth as their merit and think highly of themselves for it. The poor respect the rich as well, just because they are rich. Why is this? Because both the poor and the rich believe that wealth is worth striving for.

Pride

We can address people using different formal titles: your honor, sir, your majesty, your reverence, and so on. But there is only one true title that suits us all: brother. "Brother" reminds us that we are all brothers and sisters before God.

No one demonstrates the very essence of equality better than children. Children treat all people equally, while adults teach children to respect kings, rich people, and celebrities and to despise servants and paupers.

It is easier to get along with people when you treat them as if they are better than you, as opposed to you being better than them.

A child greets another child with a friendly and joyful smile, no matter what class, nationality, or race the other child belongs to. Why are adults different?

Judgment and Punishment

When a dog is bitten by another dog, the dog bites back. People often behave this way as well. Engaging in such behavior is appalling, but it is, in fact, less harmful than teaching others that those who mistreat us should be punished.

"An eye for an eye, a tooth for a tooth, and a life for a life" — this is not human law but a law made by animals.

When we are upset with ourselves, we do not blame ourselves, our inner self, or our own soul. Rather, we blame our behavior. We should treat others in the same way. When they do something wrong, we should blame their actions, not their souls.

Pay good for evil, and the total amount of good in this world will grow.

Violence and War

 Believing that one person can improve another person's life through force is a mistake.

Violence is the worst obstacle people can create for the arrival of the kingdom of God on earth.

Why were we given an intellect and, more importantly, love in our hearts, if we continually treat others like animals, with threats and violence?

When they asked Christ what God's law was about, He replied, "To love God and your neighbor." When they asked Him the same question again, He replied, "To treat others as you wish to be treated." This is God's law in its entirety, and Buddha and Confucius also proclaimed it. Yet if you were to ask lawmakers what the law is, they wouldn't give you a short answer. They would say instead, You have much to learn.

False Science

 People believe that the more you know, the better off you will be. Yet knowing a lot is not as important as knowing a few of the most necessary things.

Socrates said that being foolish does not mean knowing a little but rather pretending to know what is not known.

Often people will learn the sciences by simply remembering and repeating the thoughts of others — eventually looking proud and important as they stand before a blacksmith, a carpenter, or a shoemaker. I have more respect for men of the trade than for these so-called scholars.

Most people believe that humanity can be improved by constantly acquiring knowledge that can make life easier. This is not entirely true. In order to improve humanity, one must find the answers to those questions that really matter in this life. Discovering such truths is possible.

Desire and Passion

Your treasure is where your heart is. If a person believes that his or her treasure is in the body only — for example, in good food, a comfortable house, nice clothing, or other pleasures — then this person will be consumed by the pursuit of such things. Indeed, the more energy one puts into pleasing the body, the less energy one will have to invest in a spiritual life.

The desires of our bodies are like little children who always want more. The more you give in, the more they ask of you, and this goes on without end.

If you follow the desires of your flesh, you make it weaker. If you keep your flesh too strictly, you also weaken it. There is, then, only one true middle.

Anger and Hatred

In the same way as water flows from a pail with a small hole, your life will feel empty if you have hatred toward even one person.

When you are angry, count to ten before you do or say anything. If you are still angry, count to one hundred. In your silence, you will be surprised at how angry you had become over such small things.

One of the most precious things a person can do while on this earth is to experience rage without behaving as such.

If someone offends you, you can respond like a dog, a cow, or a horse: run away or bite back. Or you can act like a human being and say to yourself, "This person abused me. That is his or her choice; but my choice is to do what is good."

Effort

It is important to live according to one's own will and not the will of others. Yet, in order to do so, a person must live for his or her soul and be ready for the considerable effort this requires.

Both children and adults believe that the truth is a source of goodness. However, the truth requires one to make an effort if one is to be freed from misconceptions and lies.

You make an effort to wake yourself up from a bad dream. In the same way, you must make an effort to wake up in life and move from your animal self to your spiritual self.

Lao-tzu, a Chinese wise man, preached that doing nothing was the highest virtue. While this may seem strange at first, it becomes less so when we consider all the evil that has been done in this world.

Thoughts

We often believe that our life moves forward only when we meet others. This is not true. Our real lives unfold when we are alone, when we are one-on-one with our thoughts.

A thought is a great force. This force finds its way out of a person through words, making one's deeds a blessing or a curse, depending on whether it was a good or bad thought.

It is only after an artillery shell has left the cannon that we hear the shot from a distance. In the same way, we can see the evil created by evil thoughts only after they have been expressed and caused evil things to happen. All human action depends on our thoughts.

When it is in the soil, a seed is invisible. Yet a huge tree eventually grows from it over time. In the same way, human thoughts can go unnoticed. Yet the greatest events in human history often grow from such thoughts.

Words

Saying bad things about someone brings harm on three sides: to those about whom you speak, to those with whom you speak, and most importantly, to yourself.

Remember, a word is a deed and is different from other deeds in only one respect: we cannot always be aware of its consequences. For this reason, be very careful with your words.

An honest word has power beyond that of priests, bishops, kings, and those who are wealthy.

People learn how and what to speak, but there is a much more important science: how and when to keep silent.

A kind word is a key to a person's heart.
— CHINESE PROVERB

Truth

 We must teach our children the universal rules — the truths that unite the different nations of this world.

The truth is inherently simple and clear. A lie, however, is always complicated and requires endless words and excuses.

You can kill those who speak the truth, but once it is spoken, the truth will live forever.

A truth learned through another's assertion sticks to us as though it does not belong, like a wax nose, for example. However, a truth you discover for yourself is like a part of your own body. It belongs to you.

The greatest obstacle to understanding truth is not the lie itself, but the fact that the lie tries to look like the truth.

Humility and Modesty

 We often try to hide our vices so that others will not blame us. This is a mistake, because criticism can be useful.

All temptation comes from pride. To save yourself from temptation, be humble.

If you want to experience the true joy of a good deed, do it in secret and forget that you have done it. Only then will the good deed appear both outside and inside you.

The major task in every person's life is to become a kinder and better person. How can you become better if you think you are good enough already?

Humility offers a kind of joy that cannot be achieved by a selfish and proud person.

Self-Sacrifice

 The Bible says that those who lose their lives will find them. Thus, your real life begins only when you live for your soul and not for your body.

One's life cannot be secured, so one should be ready to die at any time. In this way, life becomes free, and one can strive for the perfection of the soul in loving other people.

There is no life without sacrifice. Your entire life involves the sacrifice of the body for the sake of the soul.

The most joyful and truthful thing in life is to nourish your soul. To do this, you must deny yourself and make sacrifices. Begin with small sacrifices to make the larger ones possible.

To improve your life, you must be ready to sacrifice it.

Prayer

 To pray is to reflect on eternal truth while comparing yourself to the truth of God.

A true prayer does not ask for favors or worldly goods but to strengthen your inner self and your good thoughts.

A true prayer is necessary for your soul, because when you speak to God in your prayer, your thoughts reach their highest.

A true prayer is support for your soul, a confession, a checkup on your past deeds, and direction for your future actions.

I want to ask for help from God. This is my prayer. Yet no one has seen God directly, so how can we talk to Him? We can talk through love. If we love others with our actions and deeds—this will be our help from God, this is our greatest blessing.

Work and Idleness

A person cannot live without work. If the human race did not work, we would eventually die of hunger and need. This we all know. If a person does not work but instead lives in luxury, he or she is taking from others the fruits of their labor.

There is nothing wrong with giving money to the poor if it was you who earned that money. A proverb says, "A dry, lazy hand is greedy; a sweaty, working hand is generous." The teachings of the Twelve Apostles say, "Let your giving to the poor be with the sweat of your hand."

Physical labor is useful because, among other things, it keeps your mind busy.

Manual labor, especially working in the soil, is useful for both your body and your soul. Not only does this labor allow your mind to rest, but it also brings you closer to nature. This is difficult for people who do not work with their hands to understand.

Love

 They asked a Chinese wise man, "What is science?" He answered, "To know people." They asked him, "What is goodness?" He answered, "To love people."

In order to live according to the law of God, a bird must fly, a fish must swim, and a person must love. If people did harm to others rather than love them, they would be behaving as strangely as if a bird were to swim or a fish were to fly.

The greatest way to improve each other's lives is not through money, gifts, good advice, or even work, but through love.

Every person's responsibility is to nurture love and bring it into this world.

Living in the Present

 We divide time into three parts: the past, the present, and the future. In reality, there is only a tiny point at which the future meets the past, and while this point may seem small, it is where our entire lives are concentrated.

Love is the most important thing of all. But one cannot love in the past or the future. One can love only now, at the present time and in the present moment.

The purpose of life is to bring forth goodness. Now, in this life.

Love is a manifestation of the divine, for which the notion of time does not exist. Therefore, love is manifested only now, in the present, in every instant.

There Is No Evil

If there were no darkness, we would not know color or light. In the same way, if there were no evil, we would not know virtue or righteousness.

There is considerable evil in this world. Yet this is not because people do not perform sufficient acts of goodness, but rather because they engage in acts that they shouldn't.

If we believed and recalled that our strength is in our thoughts, then so much evil would disappear, allowing more goodness to enter this world.

We call evil those things that bring suffering and discomfort to our bodily life. However, our life is about freeing our soul from our body. Therefore, for those who understand life as a spiritual experience, there is no evil.

Death

When we know that death is near, we must complete our unfinished business in this world. Yet there is only one thing that is always complete — our love toward other people here, in the present moment.

Death is the breaking of the vessel in which our spirit was enclosed. You should not confuse the vessel with what is inside it.

If you are afraid of death, you should remember that the fear is not in death itself, but in you. Becoming a better person means that you will fear death less. No matter what happens to you, you will always be happy if you are united with God.

One day you will realize that you have never really been born but have always lived. It is then you will realize that you will never die.

After Death

 We often think that life lasts between the time of our birth and the time of our death. This is similar to thinking that a pond is without a shoreline, and that when the water flows away, it disappears.

If you love God with all your soul, then you know your life does not end with your death.

They asked a wise man about eternal life: "What will happen to us when this world comes to an end?" He answered, "I do not need the world, and I am not afraid of its end, because I know that my soul is eternal."

God is eternal, all-embracing, and exists across space and time. God is all there is. All exists in Him. All life, when it appears, does not come from nothing, but rather from God. And when death takes us, it does not take us to nothing; it takes us to God.

Life Is a Blessing

 Everything is given to us. If you look properly and seek goodness in those places where it truly exists — in the unification of your soul with God — then you will have everything you need.

Life is the highest blessing possible. We often neglect the joy of this life, expecting that someday, somewhere, we can secure a better blessing. But there can be no better one than this — here, in your everyday life.

Your true blessing is within your own hands. Like a shadow, it follows a good life.

If your life does not seem like a limitless blessing and a limitless joy, then it is moving in the wrong direction.

Try to live your life in such a way that if it should end soon, the time left would be an unexpected gift.

Happiness

 The source of true happiness is in your heart. It would be foolish to look for it elsewhere. You would be like the shepherd looking for a lost lamb when all along it was tucked inside his shirt.

The first rule of wisdom is to know thyself. However, this is the most difficult thing to do. The first rule of virtue is to be happy with little things; this, too, is hard to do. Only those people who follow these rules can be strong enough to be a virtuous example for others.

If you love only yourself, you cannot be truly happy. Live for others, and then you will find true happiness.

Where are you wandering, unhappy people? Looking for a better life? You are running away, but happiness is to be found inside you. If it is not within, then it is nowhere else. Happiness is in your ability to love others.

Love

From birth until death, you want to be well, and that is given to you. It is easy to find such goodness if you look in the proper places, that is, by loving God and all other people.

In order to be happy, you need do only one thing: love others. Love everyone, both kind and evil people. Love without stopping, and then you will have constant blessings and happiness.

As soon as you concentrate your life in the unification of love with all living creatures and with God, then your life will change at once from tortures and suffering to happiness and blessings.

The will of God is fulfilled whether you follow it or not. On you depends only whether you resist it or fill yourself with it in the form of love — and thereby receive a limitless blessing.

The kingdom of God is inside you. Your blessing is inside your heart if your heart is filled with love.

Faith

 The law of God is to do what God wants us to do, and not to do what He does not want us to.

True religion is not believing in a supernatural event or following rules and rituals. True religion is the attitude a person has toward others and the limitless world, an attitude based on intelligence and contemporary knowledge.

Different faiths and religions have many different changing laws and rules and also some that are changeless and eternal. These eternal laws are the true religion.

When someone says you live in lies and they live in the truth — this is the cruelest statement a person can make. Yet people who speak about religion often use these exact words.

Those who place religion second in their lives have no religion at all.

Soul

There are two paths in life: one is to live for the body, the other for the spirit. If you live for the body, it will become clear that bodily pleasures are fragile, weaken over the years, and end with death. If you live for the spirit, on the other hand, the joys of life will multiply with time, and death will no longer be something to fear.

Who are we then? Nothing. Indeed, we are nothing. But this "nothing" is able to understand itself and its place in this world.

When you look at yourself as a material being, you become an unsolvable puzzle to yourself. As soon as you understand that your inner "me" is the spirit enclosed in your body, the puzzle disappears, and the world becomes easy to comprehend.

If we compare our physical force with the forces of nature — we are nothing. If we look at our spirit, which is part of the divine spirit, we understand that we are something above the rest of this world.

One Soul in All

The majority think that only they are important and others are not. There are, however, kind and clever people who understand that the lives of others and animals are as important as their own, and genuinely care about others. For such people, living and dying is easy.

There was a time when all people ate human meat and thought they were doing nothing wrong. Now, more and more people understand that it is bad to eat the meat of animals. The time will come when all people think killing and eating sheep, cows, or pigs is as bad as slaying a man.

All living creatures, humans and animals, are closely connected. When one suffers, the others suffer too. In the same way, when one is happy, the happiness spreads and makes others happy.

You will understand this life only when you will see yourself in every person.

God

 Do not look for God in the temples. He is inside of you, living within. Surrender to God, and you will always be joyful and happy.

A thinking person can feel the presence of his own spirit and the universal spirit — God. But as soon as he tries to clarify and explain these ideas, he humbly has to stop, and cannot touch the veil that covers them. All nations preach the great superior Spirit, calling it different names and dressing it in different clothes. Underneath these names and clothes, there is only one God.
— JEAN-JACQUES ROUSSEAU

The one who guides our lives and the lives of the whole world is God.

God desires good for all. If you wish for goodness for all as well, then God lives in you.

One can avoid saying the name of God, but one cannot avoid accepting His existence. Nothing exists if He does not exist.

Unification in Spirit

When a person lives only for his body, it seems only one thing exists and is important: "me." However, there are millions who wish to be happy as individuals and who contradict each other, for no one is completely satisfied. Your "me" tells you that your body is not eternal and will disappear and die with time. The way out of this contradiction is accepting that your "self" is not in body alone but in spirit, which spirit will be united with others by love, as there is no death for the spirit.

The body wants what is best for itself, even if it harms the spirit. The spirit wants what is best for itself, even if it harms the body. This struggle disappears only when you understand that your life is not in the body, which will disappear and die, but the body is just a place where your eternal soul temporarily abides.

A person can understand how good love is when he understands how fragile his body is.

Universal Love

If you expect a reward for your love, it is not true love. The essential quality of love is to give blessings to all who are around you without asking for something in return.

People live not by what they think about life but only through love.

You want goodness, and you will receive it when you desire goodness for all.

There is a lot of goodness in this world, but there is only one true good: loving other people.

Love that is given for a reason is not pure love. Only unlimited, unconditional love is eternal. Such love does not disappear but grows continuously with time.

Sin

There is no life without sin and redeeming your mistakes. Our sins are like an eggshell or a grain of wheat. Getting rid of your sins is like breaking the outer shell, which frees the chick or germ to grow as it is exposed to fresh air and light. In the same way, our spiritual self grows when exposed to God's spirit.

Your body should serve your soul. But often, owing to circumstance, the opposite happens. This is what I call a sin.

In the spiritual world, all is more closely connected than in the material world. Any lie leads to several more lies, any cruelty to several other cruelties.

Children seem purer to us than adults, most likely because their minds have not yet been spoiled by the prejudices of the adults. Adults have to contend with their sin.

Temptation

Serve your body only when it needs it, not by creating more ways to please it. When you please your body too much, you are in fact hurting yourself. To have a good life, your body should serve your spirit, not the other way around.

You can suffer only with your body; your spirit knows no suffering. The weaker your spiritual life, the more you will suffer. It is best to live more by your spirit.

Your stomach acts like shackles on the hands and feet of your spirit. You should eat to combat hunger, not for pleasure.

The less attention you pay to food, expensive clothes, and entertainment, the more freedom you will have.

Work and Idleness

 If you do not want to work, you will live either by humiliation or violence, or by stealing from others.

We should respect people not according to their wealth but for the work they do. It often happens that lazy but very rich people are respected, while those who perform useful but physical work, such as farmers or laborers, are not. This is wrong.

Nothing harms a good life more than neglecting simple, everyday work — making your own food, cleaning your house, and doing your laundry. Many rich people neglect such chores, but to an honest person this is the most important work of his life.

If you work for other people, do not be ashamed of this and do not ask for extra pay. Remember that your labor, when done in love for the goodness of others, is good for your spirit.

Desire and Passion

People often don't distinguish between the two kinds of love, physical and spiritual. If you cannot see any difference, you cannot see the difference between lies and the truth.

Jesus taught the following about sexual relationships, "You have heard it said, 'Do not commit adultery.' But I tell you that anyone who looks at a woman lustfully has already committed adultery with her in his heart" (Matthew 5:27–28). According to this teaching, a person should strive for celibacy, and by doing so you are doing what is best.

It is sinful to look at food only as a source of pleasure. Similarly, it is sinful to look at sex as being only for your pleasure. This is harmful to your soul.

We can say that the desire for marriage and children exists in some people to the degree that they cannot fulfill the law of God and hope their children will.

41

Sin

 Bodily sins, such as gluttony, laziness, and lust, are bad in their own right but also because they lead to hostility between people.

If you want to be loved by everyone, you should not pay too much attention to material goods, for you cannot have all that other people have. Instead you should put your love in spiritual blessings — the things that many can have at the same time.

Don't despise or praise others. If you despise them, you will not see the good in them. If you praise them too highly, your expectations for them will be too great. Show respect for others, as they do for you.

Buddhists say that every sin is the result of stupidity. This is true for all sins, especially hate and hostility toward others.

Pride

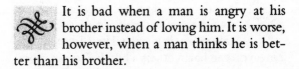 It is bad when a man is angry at his brother instead of loving him. It is worse, however, when a man thinks he is better than his brother.

It is foolish when one person thinks himself superior to another person. It is even more foolish when one nation thinks itself superior to another nation.

Just as a person cannot lift himself into the air, so he cannot truly glorify himself.

You can treat others with superiority only in your physical life. However, if you live a spiritual life, you will see all people as being equal to yourself.

Inequality is not compatible with true love. Love is the sun shining equally on all people. If the sun shone for some and not for others, it would not be the sun, nor true love.

Vanity and Fame

It is dangerous to live only for fame. If you live for yourself alone, you harm only yourself if you falter. If you live for fame, you can harm others a hundred times more.

Be indifferent to other people's opinions about you. Without indifference, you cannot be a free man.

Most sins and temptations grow weaker over the years as you age. However, you will have to struggle with the sin of vanity from childhood to old age.

God created heaven and earth, but we cannot grasp this concept or find happiness in it. God also created us to understand happiness. We were all created as a part of one body, a body that must love itself.

Greed and Wealth

 A compassionate man is never rich. A rich man is not compassionate.
— CHINESE PROVERB

Some people say, "I am rich because I am better than others," and at the same time say, "I am better than others because I am rich." Yes, it is truly difficult for a rich man to enter the kingdom of God.

You should amass the kind of wealth and riches that no one can take from you, that remain with you even after death and never go away. Such riches are stored in your spirit, in a life filled with love.

Ten good, decent men can lie down in a small room and have good night's sleep on a floor covered with a simple blanket. However, two rich men cannot tolerate each other even in a mansion with ten bedrooms.

Over time, the rich become more ashamed and the poor more desperate.

45

Pride

In ancient times, even in the Middle Ages, people believed that not all nationalities were equal, and some, such as the Persians, Greeks, Romans, or French, were better than others. We can no longer believe this.

Only children evidence true equality among people. Adults commit a crime when they teach children to treat others unequally.

Nationalism is a prejudice based on the inequality of peoples.

Servants in the homes of the rich constitute an absurdity that contradicts Christianity.

People who preach morality often limit their responsibility to their family or country, but in doing so they teach selfishness. Family and country are only two circles enclosed in the wider circle of humanity.

Judgment and Punishment

 Revenge and punishment for those who have abused or harmed you in any way is a mistake, as is the teaching that violence is useful to men.

Violence can be an obstacle and a hindrance to what people want. However, like a dam that cannot halt the flow of a river, violence cannot stop the tide of emotions that will one day be released.

Everyone understands that evil cannot destroy evil. We only increase it when we believe people must be punished for doing something wrong. We don't get rid of evil but multiply it when we return evil for evil.

We can see the sin in others the same way we see dirt on their faces, but we cannot see our own sins because we are not looking in the mirror of our conscience. We need to look into that mirror more often. Then we would blame others less for their sins, and become purer.

Violence and War

It seems a simple matter to change society and make people better. So, we often try to change those around us and forget about our own spiritual growth, our striving for inner perfection. The only real way to improve society is to improve your spiritual self.

Many prejudices, mistaken beliefs, false attitudes, and empty rituals tell us how to serve God. There is also the prejudice that some can force their views about how to live a good life on others and tell them what to do.

To change society without the inner improvement of each individual is like trying to rebuild a stone house by just shuffling and rearranging the stones without using mortar to bind them. No matter which way you arrange the stones, if they aren't cemented together, the whole building will fall apart in bad weather.

The improvement of this world lies in replacing violence with love, and in understanding that the basis for a beautiful life is not the fear of violence but love.

Work and Idleness

Nothing hinders the life of people more than some making others do as they wish by force. The day will come when people will understand that there is a common law, not the law of violence but universal love for each other.

— FÉLICITÉ ROBERT DE LAMENNAIS

Thieves live by stealing. You cannot believe they are decent people until they stop, and prayer and sacrifices will not make them good. The same is true of the rich and the lazy. If they do not work but rely on the labor of others, they cannot be good either, no matter how much they pray or sacrifice.

Those who encourage the division of labor take the easiest work for themselves. It is strange, though, that their managerial work becomes arduous while the physical work they avoid becomes the most pleasurable.

The greatest gifts can be destroyed by idleness. — MICHEL DE MONTAIGNE

Truth

 Our life became bad, even worse, than the life of the pagans, because we accepted false truth instead of the real truth.

No sooner did people decide they could create an organization called a church, and in doing so were free of sin, than another group of people appeared, saying the same thing. As soon as these groups started accusing each other of telling lies, it became likely that both were wrong.

Any slavery is easier to bear than slavery based on false religion. A person who is a slave to a certain sect or church is under the complete control of his masters.

Our age is the age of practical criticism, where everything can be critically examined and evaluated.

Two groups try to hide from criticism. Religious institutions hide under the pretext of being saintly, and lawmakers hide under the pretext of their power and greatness. — IMMANUEL KANT

False Science

Owls can see in the dark but become blind in bright light. The same is true of many scholars. They know many unnecessary scholarly trifles but do not know, or want to know, the most important science needed for life — how you should live in this world.

Just as there are false views on everything, there are false sciences. Some ideas are taken to be the only truth, not because of people's needs but because scholars deem it necessary. Science then becomes false. This happens often in our world.

The ability of the mind to absorb knowledge is not unlimited. Therefore, you should not believe the more you know, the better. The knowledge of many unimportant things is an obstacle to true knowledge.

Effort

When a person seeks to improve himself, he may fall back on his old ways but eventually always returns to his efforts. This step back is always smaller than his progress forward. If a person wants to improve his inner life, he will eventually succeed.

We should rid ourselves of the mistaken view that heaven can fix our sins. No one can do this for you but yourself. If you cook a meal in a careless, sloppy way, you don't expect God to make it tasty. If you take a wrong direction in life, you shouldn't expect God, through divine intervention, to change it and suddenly make it better.   — JOHN RUSKIN

To say you cannot make an effort to keep from doing what is wrong is the same as admitting you are not a human being but an animal or a lifeless object. Humans know that it is within our power to make an effort.

Every religion teaches us that all our life is an effort, progressing from the basic animal stages to the higher life of the spirit.

There Is No Evil

If one iota of the effort people put into getting rich, entertaining themselves, or arguing were invested in improving their inner self and not fighting their conscience, soon all the evil would disappear from this world.

Do not tell or complain about the bad things your loved ones have done. If others gossip, judge, and criticize their neighbors, try to ignore it. The less you judge others, the better it will be for you.

You cannot increase the goodness of this life. Your life in itself is a good thing. All you have to do is not spoil it. We do live bad lives sometimes, but this is because we did bad things that we shouldn't have done.

The words, "*Aut bene, aut nihil*," are understood to mean, "About the dead say only good, or say nothing." This is wrong. One should say the opposite: "About the living say only good, or say nothing." Doing this would save us from many mistakes and from mixing up what is good with what is evil.

Thoughts

 You cannot physically eliminate sin, temptation, or lies. You can eliminate them only in your thoughts.

The spiritual force that moves this world often slips from our attention. It is not found in books, newspapers, the law, or scholarly journals. Invisible, it is always free. It can be found in your thoughts, and is the force of your spirit.

First speak with your inner voice when thinking about this world; only then should you speak to other people.

Just as the lives of men are defined not by their actions but by the inner thoughts guiding their actions, the same can be said about entire nations. They are defined not by the outer events but by the shared ideas that unite people.

One great thought lodged in the soul of a man can change his whole life.

Truth

 Do not believe anything on someone's word alone. Think and analyze everything, then accept only those things approved by your intellect.

To live a good life, live by the truth and look for guidance from those wise people who lived before us.

The truth comes to you only if you use your intelligence.

If you want to know the truth, free yourself from all thoughts of personal profit, and then make your decision.

Every person seeking truth reminds me of a farmer. His main task is to select the truth, as a farmer selects his best seeds, and then plant this truth, as the farmer plants his seeds in the soil. Words are your major tools.

Humility and Modesty

 Truly virtuous people do not think they are virtuous, because they *are*.

True virtue does not speak about itself or show off. False virtue wants to strut and boast.

Humble, clever people with good morals usually respect loud, blustering people without morals. This is because a humble and clever person judges others according to his own standards and cannot imagine how a stupid idea can be said with so much self-confidence.

Humility is the basis of all virtue and intellect. There is no thought more useful than thinking you are just a small insect, a tiny particle, nothing.

If you only understood you were a small and unimportant person, you would not fear death, and you would have true joy in life.

Self-Sacrifice

 The less you pay attention to your body, the more you will gain in your spiritual life. You have to choose what is more important to you.

The one thing that does not cease is living only for others. When you live for others, you can live a happy and quiet life.

To have true faith, you should deny yourself. To deny yourself, you need faith. These two things reinforce each other.

Times moves on, and the riddle of how man can live a good life remains an unsolvable puzzle — yet it was solved long ago.

A person must be willing to sacrifice bodily life for spiritual life.

Living in the Present

Your life here in the present is the time when God lives in us. Therefore, a minute of your life in the present is more precious than anything else. Try with all your might not to waste this time, and look carefully for the manifestation of God within you.

The older I become, the clearer my memories. It is strange how I remember only the good and kind things and can enjoy these memories sometimes even more than I enjoy the present. What does this mean? That nothing goes away. Nothing was or will be, for everything is here, now, in the present.

If you live your whole life into the present, you will have no questions about your future life, before or after death.

Effort

To move from our animal to our spiritual being, we need to fight evil. Only by overcoming our problems, misfortunes, and suffering do we grow closer to our spiritual self.

They say that those who are lucky in life, who are rich, healthy, and don't have the usual problems, are often bad and weak. From this, you see why a person needs to make an effort in life to overcome obstacles. We should not complain about our difficulties but surmount them.

A human is part of the spirit of God enclosed in a body. At the beginning of life, a person does not think this, believing his life is found in his body. The longer he lives, the more he understands that his true life is found not in the body but in the spirit.

If you have an enemy, use him to learn how to forgive and love your enemies. You will acquire more this way than you would have if you simply shut him out.

Death

 If life is a dream and death is an awakening, then in my future dream I can see myself as another, different being.

Humans, like animals, resist death, but, because of their intelligence, even though they resist they may agree with its necessity.

All human life is comprised of innumerable small changes that are invisible to our eye but happen to us every minute. At the very beginning of these changes, we were a child. At the very end comes death, which is not for us to understand. Death is the change of the form in which our spirit lives. We should not confuse the form with what is connected to it.

Our life, from birth to death, including our dreams — is it not all just one big dream, which we think of as one real life, with a greater life still ahead of us?

Faith

Every person feels that there is something great inside him or her. In life, that something — that which cannot be understood — is the most important thing of all. A person's attitude toward that thing is religion.

True religious law is so clear and simple that people have no excuse not to know it.

An expert in the law tested him with this question: "Teacher, which is the greatest commandment in the Law?" Jesus replied, "Love the Lord your God with all your heart and with all your soul and with all your mind. This is the first and greatest commandment. And the second is like it: Love your neighbor as yourself. All the Law and the Prophets hang on these two commandments."   — MATTHEW 22:35-36

Trust in the power of the intellect is the foundation of every faith. One cannot believe in God if one underestimates the ability of the very intellect through which one understands God.

Soul

A person feels good, big, and important when comparing him or herself to an insect. Yet, when compared to the size of the earth, he or she feels small. When compared to the sun, the earth is but a tiny piece of sand. When compared to other big stars, the sun, too, is tiny. What is a person's body when compared to the sun and the stars above? Nothing.

People sometimes ask, "Have you forgotten about God?" This is a good question. To forget about God means to forget about the one who is always inside you. To remember God — and to do this not only through words but also by constantly remembering that God lives in us — is truly a great thing.

If you understand yourself as a spiritual being, you can save yourself from all troubles. No matter what happens to you, you will be untouchable.

One Soul in All

 If a person understands that he or she lives not by the body but by the spirit, then he or she will feel a sense of unity with all living creatures.

One cannot find the origin of our souls here on earth, nor in the ability to remember the past, understand the present, or look into the future. We are different from the material world — we have spirits.

Feeling compassion toward all living creatures is essential to becoming a virtuous person. One cannot say, "He is a virtuous man, but he is not compassionate," or "This is a compassionate man, but he is cruel." These phrases simply do not make sense.

In order to get along well with other people, you must contemplate those things that unite you, not those that separate you.

God

When you look up at the clear winter sky, you see star after star, seemingly without end. And when you realize that each of those stars is many times bigger than the earth, and that behind those stars are thousands, maybe millions, of even bigger stars, and that the sky has no end, you realize you cannot even begin to comprehend it all. These are the things that you call God.

A person cannot help but think there is something behind his or her life, that he or she is somebody's tool made for a particular purpose. The someone, or something, that uses this tool is God.

God is eternal, all-embracing, and exists across space and time. God is all there is. There is no other God than this God. All exists in Him. All life, when it appears, does not come from nothing, but rather, from God. And when death takes us, it does not take us to nothing, it takes us back to God.

Unification in Spirit

You can understand your life in two ways. The first is to believe that you are the most important person, and that all other people, animals, and living beings are secondary to you; they simply live around you. It is when you live like this that you feel anger toward others.

However, there is a second way to understand your life: that the entire world lives the same way you do and that you are united with all. Only then will you feel good inside, with your soul at ease.

You might say one day, "I feel bored and lonely." But who told you to forget about those around you while locking yourself in a prison called "me"?

A person can live a good life only when he or she understands him- or herself as a spiritual being, a being united with all.

Universal Love

 We can improve each other's lives not through money, gifts, good advice, or even work, but through love.

One should not be afraid of God because God *is* love. How can one be afraid of love? If one loves God, one cannot be afraid of anything in this world.

God created heaven and earth, which cannot find joy in the fact of their existence. Then God created thinking creatures that can find such joy. We were all created as if we were a single body, a body that must love itself.

Love — not toward a particular person but rather a spiritual love for all — that is the state within which we can understand our own spirit, our soul.

Sin

 Our life is spent struggling against sin, temptation, and prejudice.

There are five major sins that torture people: gluttony, sloth, lust, anger or animosity, and finally, pride.

If our bodies were not separate from each other, the divine spirit within us would be united. Without the body, there can be no life, but another life exists apart from the body.

Every sin comes from a lack of knowledge.

If you can rise above your rage and anger, and forgive and be kind to those who have harmed you, you are doing the best a person is capable of.

Desire and Passion

In their physical life, especially when reproducing, people should be higher than animals, not below them. When animals copulate, they do so to have babies. Men and women form sexual relationships to have a good time, often with no thought of children.

When a man and a woman are physically intimate and do not plan to have children together, they commit a sin.

Only the sin of lust grows in the imagination. Try to rid yourself of these thoughts, and remember your spiritual inner being.

Whether it is good to give birth or not, we do not know. The one who created this world knew what He was doing. We should keep this in mind when we violate the virtue of celibacy and fall into sexual sin.

Temptation

You can always determine what your body truly needs to survive: clothing and a piece of bread to eat. But your body craves more and more without end, and when you give in to it, you can never satisfy its desires.

If you fail to meet your body's requirements for food, sleep, or rest from work, your body immediately sets about showing you your mistake. However, if you spend too much time in idleness, the mistake will only surface in the future, when you grow weak and fall out of the habit of working.

Socrates, a wise man, tried to abstain from every excessive thing. He ate only to satisfy his hunger, not to develop sophisticated tastes, and asked his students to do the same and spend more time improving their spirit.

When you concentrate your efforts in your body and not on your spiritual growth, you are like a bird walking on its weak legs instead of flying where it wants on its powerful wings.

Greed and Wealth

It is understandable that the rich, who have accumulated enormous wealth, think of their wealth as their greatest accomplishment, for they sacrificed a great deal to get it. However, it is strange that the poor respect the rich for this. Why do they? The poor respect and admire the rich, because they desire the same for themselves.

Did God give something to one person, and not give it to everyone? Did our Eternal Father exclude any of his children? Show me where it says in the New Testament that our Heavenly Father left anyone out.

— Félicité Robert de Lamennais

Riches never satisfy. The more you have, the more you want to have to assuage your appetite. Even the greatest of riches cannot satisfy the person seeking more and more wealth.

The injustice of large property is bound up with many other injustices and sins that exist to support enormous wealth.

Work and Idleness

 Do not bother another person asking for things you can do yourself.

If man does not contend with nature, his body will decay and die. And if man shuns his duty by forcing someone else to do it for him, then his soul, too, will decay and die.

Some people think manual labor will prevent you from having an intellectual life. On the contrary, you can have an intellectual *and* spiritual life only if you engage in manual labor.

When you work with your hands, you study the world around you. When I go to my vegetable garden and dig with my spade, I always think: "Why did I not create this by myself, so as to be as happy as I am now?" Because it *also* required good health and knowledge.

I am ashamed in front of my woodcutter, my baker, and my cook, because they have the ability to satisfy themselves; they can live without my help for a day, or even a year. As for me, I must depend on them.   — RALPH WALDO EMERSON

Anger and Hatred

It is difficult to be kind to an evil or immoral person, especially if he abuses you. Yet it is especially to this type of person that you should show kindness, both for his sake and your own.

A clever person knows that all he needs is within him, and wants to keep on improving himself. A stupid person wants others to treat him nicely, and grows angry if they do not give him what he wants. A clever person has no one to be angry at.

Very often, we do not notice the good that people do. We simply do not see it because we dislike them, and this is our mistake. To overcome this hard feeling, change your attitude and try to see the best in people you do not love.

Just as dust thrown into the wind returns to the person who threw it, evil returns to those who commit evil.
— INDIAN PROVERB

Pride

A proud person wants the praise of others. To be praised, he must be admired by people. To be admired, people must like him. To like him, people must think well of him. However, people don't think highly of the proud, so a proud person never gets what he wants.

It is stupid to be proud. However, it is even stupider to be proud of your family background, or your nationality.

Most evil in this world comes from pride. One family fights another, and a war between nations may follow.

A proud person seems as though covered in a shell of ice. No good feeling can penetrate.

Vanity and Fame

We should live like the miners who were isolated in a mineshaft after an earthquake. You do the best you can and try not to think about the opinion of others. Such is real life.

Living for God, not people, seems difficult because you do not perceive a material reward for your good life. But the truth is the opposite. God's spirit, living inside you, will reward you instantly, and this spiritual reward is better than anything anyone else can give you.

A flatterer flatters you because he has a low opinion of you. So why do you listen to him and rejoice in his praise?

One who pays too much attention to what other people say about him will never find peace.

Judgment and Punishment

When something bad is done to you, you want revenge, but in making up explanations and excuses, you say you want to improve the person who hurt you.

Those who think you cannot rule without violence and threats are like horses wearing blinders so they can pull their load without being distracted.

In our attempt to oppose evil, we actually commit more evil when we apply punishment as our response.

Our life is far from a Christian one. We can see this in the belief that punishment is a good and useful tool in bringing up children. The law of Christ may tell us to forgive and not reply to evil with evil: we think this is a joke and continue to do the opposite.

Every punishment is cruel. The punishment of our day, prison, is as cruel as the lashes of a whip a hundred years ago.

Effort

There is only one way to improve society, which is for all of us to improve ourselves. For this to happen, you need do only one thing: improve your inner self.

Our life's improvement and our fight against evil can begin only with the spiritual development of each individual.

It would be revealing to take a poll of so-called educated people on how we should improve our life. There would be such a great divergence in their answers that it would show the impossibility of improving others' lives. The only way to improve this world is through your own spiritual self-improvement.

It is clear that we will be defeated in our physical life, and we will have to die. We see this with our own eyes and our intellect. This is the law of the world that God wills. The person who understands this stops struggling for the fruits of his physical life and devotes more effort to his spiritual life.

Violence and War

People follow judicial laws and regulations more precisely than the law of God. This should not be, for the laws in one country differ from those of other countries, while God's law is the same for everyone everywhere.

Government not only has actual power but the false teachings that support this power.

The only way to eliminate violence is not to participate in it.

The sword and the rifle, the weapons of our day, will be exhibited in museums of the future as artifacts of ancient times, just as we now view the medieval weapons of the Inquisition.

Faith

Christ was asked, "What is the real law?" He said, "Love God and your neighbor." The same thought was taught by Buddha and Confucius.

As a rule, parents raise their children for our present-day world. However, we should be raising our children for their future life, so they can live in better conditions and make this world a better place.

It does not take a lot of mental effort to understand kindness. I ask myself just one question: Can I agree that the motives for my actions could be a universal law for all?

God gives us faith in our hearts and the help of our conscience and our intellect. We cannot build faith in other people through threats and force. So let us not blame the lost and unbelievers; they are already unhappy enough from their own mistaken ways.

False Science

 The most passionate defenders of science lack a profound knowledge of any one particular science.
— GEORGE C. LICHTENBERG

The greatest thinkers of the past were great because they freely expressed their own thoughts and did not simply repeat what others had written in books.
— RALPH WALDO EMERSON

Today, science occupies the place the institution of the church occupied two hundred to three hundred years ago. Both hold similar meetings, conferences, and synods. Both offer the same lack of critical thinking, key concepts that are both broad and vague, and self-confident pride.

You need to know a lot to understand how little you know.

Effort

We live to be free of sin. The greater the effort, the more goodness you will achieve. Therefore, what is good about a person is their effort to become better.

Confront every obstacle that interferes with your ability to love.

Very often, our body wants one thing, but our spirit wants something different. Our body wants to eat, but our spirit wants to give food away to the hungry. Which should you choose?

Pay attention to everything you do, and do not think anything unworthy of your attention.
— CONFUCIUS

We always feel good when we do good for other people. If we live for others, the entire world becomes our friend.

Self-Sacrifice

 The person who cannot see himself in his dying body knows the wisdom of this life. — BUDDHIST PROVERB

You cannot separate yourself from humanity even if you want to. You live in it, for it, and together with it. We are all created for interaction and communication with each other, but this is impossible without self-denial.
— MARCUS AURELIUS

Loving yourself excessively can become an illness of the spirit. In its most pronounced form, it can become a mental illness, called "mania grandiose."

Do you want others to live for you and to love you more than they love themselves? There is only one way for your wish to come true: for all creatures to live for the good of all others and to love everyone. Only then will people be loved by all, and can you receive the life you desire.

Effort

Everyone knows that you cannot accomplish anything material without effort. The same applies to the major purpose of life, the life of your spirit. You can achieve nothing for your spirit without effort.

Being dissatisfied with yourself and having a desire for inner perfection are necessary conditions for your intellectual life. Only these conditions will cause you to seek to improve yourself.

After a very hot day in the middle of summer, a pleasant, refreshing rain falls to the earth. In the same way, afer the scorching sun of self-admiration, humble ways refresh the soul.

Every time you compare your actions to others', you allow temptation to place an obstacle on the path to self-improvement.

Truth

 A word of truth is more precious than all riches of the world.

No matter how tempting the lie, it will torture the person who said it. Sooner or later, a person needs to turn away from his lies and find his salvation in the truth.

When you live around other people, it is difficult to rid yourself of childhood lies and misconceptions, or those of the people you live near. You can do this only when you are by yourself. In these moments of solitude, you must question every thought and teaching you are unsure of.

If you are afraid to face the truth for your own good, you will never improve your situation but make it worse.

Words and Actions

Here you said a bad word; there you did a bad deed. Sometimes you fail to notice your words and deeds, good or bad. Let us do good deeds and speak good words, which will cause a huge tree of love to grow.

If you are unsure, abstain from both speech and action. This is a very important rule to follow.

Small, good deeds help build your character, so there are no small things in this life. All life is built from small, unimportant events and insignificant things.

To achieve something, you need to make an effort. The most difficult, and also the most important, effort is to abstain from talking.

Listen, be attentive, and speak only a little.
— SUFI WISDOM

Judgment and Punishment

 Do not judge others. If someone judges you and says bad things about you, do not judge that person in return.

The primary goal of human life is to be united with the spirit of God. Words are one of the tools that aid us in our goal. Be careful not to misuse words, and respect all kinds of words — your own, and others' judgments, written, printed, and spoken. Beware of the words that separate, and use those that unite.

Do not blame your neighbor until you put yourself in his place.

Every person who commits evil is already punished by his conscience. If he is not already suffering inside, the physical punishment he receives from others will not correct him, but only serve to make him angrier.

Thoughts

Most of the evil deeds committed by people are committed not because people are evil but because they believe in evil ideas expressed by others. We must *never* take others' ideas for granted.

If we believe and remember that our strength is in our thoughts, then so much evil would disappear, allowing goodness to enter this world.

A feeling appears independently of a person's will. But a thought can either accept or reject that feeling. Therefore, our thoughts are the essence of all things.

Our thoughts are like guests. We are not to blame for the kinds of guests we have, whether good or bad. But it is within our power to get rid of bad thoughts and to keep only those that are good.

There Is No Evil

 A person can escape the unhappiness that befalls him but not the unhappiness he creates himself.

Everyone has his problems in life, but if we live with humility, it is easy to carry this burden. Our problems are given to us so we can strive against them.

If you are ill, endure; if you are judged, respond with kindness. If you are humiliated, be humble; if you are to die, accept death with gratitude.

All truly great things happen through suffering.

A bad mood is bad not just for you but because it is contagious. If you feel unhappy, spend some time on your own. Be around others only when you're feeling better.

Living in the Present

 When you wake, ask yourself the question, "What good can I do today?"

A person planted a seed in the ground. He worried about when it would start to grow, so he removed the soil from over it and checked on it constantly. In doing so, he damaged the seed, and it didn't bear fruit. In the same way, you should work without stopping, without looking back, and the fruit of your labor will arrive when the time is right.

There is no time. There is only a tiny instant of time in the present, where all our life is concentrated. Therefore, you must focus all your efforts on this present moment.

We cannot imagine our life after death and cannot remember our life before birth, because we cannot imagine beyond the concept of time. However, our true life is outside of time.

Death

The person who does not think about eternity does not think about life. If a person were only a physical being, his death would be something pitiful. But if a person is a spiritual being, only temporarily living in his body, then death is just a change he will go through.

Remembering death does not mean living constantly with the thought of death on your mind, but being joyful and ready when one day it comes to you.

An animal lives without knowing he will die, and so does not fear death. Why then does a person anticipate his end and fear it? A wise person transfers his life from his physical to his spiritual self. This does not destroy the fear of death but makes you feel like a wanderer returning home from a long journey.

Truth/After Death

 Truth is always within your reach. It follows you as a shadow follows a person walking in sunlight.

False teachings would have it that life is evil and goodness can be attained only in a future life. The truth is that the purpose of this life is goodness, which can be achieved here and now.

Do not say that in order for you to live a good life, goodness needs to be all around you. You should make the effort to live according to God's law; then your life will be good.

If paradise is not within you, you cannot enter paradise.

Life and death are two limits. There is something similar behind them that is unknown to me; there, there is not "nothing" but "something."

Love

 Do not search for pleasures; rather, be prepared to find pleasure in all that you do. — JOHN RUSKIN

Life without love is useless. The blessings of joy are given to people only when, by resisting sin and temptation, they surrender to the godly love that lives in their spirit.

Our life is constantly moving toward that which is good.

To love is to show goodness. We all understand this love and cannot understand it otherwise. But love is not found only in words, but in the actions we perform for the sake of others.

Forget about the small and unimportant "me," stop wanting good only for yourself. Stop placing blame on others, stop feeling jealous, stop doing bad things, and you will feel God awakening in you, and beginning to shine inside you.

Faith

It is often said or thought that it is difficult to fulfill the law of God. This is not true. God does not ask you for anything other than to love God and your neighbor, and love is not difficult but joyful.

Religious thinking develops over time. It is a mistake to suppose that past religious thinking is the same as today's. This is the same as thinking that you can fit into your baby clothes again after you've grown up.

True faith does not need great temples, golden ornaments, or organ music. On the contrary, true faith comes into your heart out of silence and solitude.

Faith does not consist in the things you hesitate to believe in, but in those things you are certain of.

True religion, true faith, makes us sons of God, not His slaves. To know God means to love God, to rely on Him, and to live according to His law.

Soul

 A man lives through his spirit, not by denying his body at the same time.

All our troubles come from the fact that we forget that God lives within us.

My understanding of my spiritual life is the beginning of everything.

We cannot have a kind and happy life without believing in the existence of an eternal, timeless life.

There is not life in a body without its spirit. A body lives through it. If it seems to you that you live through your body alone, then you don't know what life is all about. And to live a good life, you must live through your spirit.

One Soul in All

 When you talk to someone, look carefully into his or her eyes. You will sense that we are all very close to one another, as if we were family, as if we had known each other for a long, long time. Why? Because the same spirit lives in all of us.

People eat animals because false teachings permit it. But your inner voice speaks to you louder than any lesson in any book, and it says you must not kill animals. This is written in our hearts.

Confucius, a Chinese wise man, said that nothing is more important than to respect other people as you respect yourself and treat others as you would like to be treated.

We are separated from each other by our bodies, but we are united by our spirit. We can feel energy waves from a distance in the spiritual world, just as we see the light of a distant star.

God

 It is good to fear God, but it is better to love God. The best is to grasp that God is inside you.

What is God? God is an eternal being and is in everything I feel part of. We all come to God sooner or later, whether we want to or not. Therefore, God exists inevitably for every person.

When you understand yourself as a separate being, then you understand other people. When you understand that everything is connected, then you understand God. We have the ability to understand both.

Through love, that is, by expanding one's limits, a human being can become closer to God. Love is not just a quality of God but also an ability in humans.

We all have thoughts and feelings we want to share with others. You may feel it's impossible, that no one else will understand, but you still have to share. Such things can only be shared with God.

Unification in Spirit

 The longer a person lives, the more he is connected with other people. The same can be said of mankind. The more the human race lives, the more united we become.

As soon as you rid yourself of egotistical love, you unwittingly unite with others.

If we did not neglect the most important teaching of Christ — unification — then we, without speaking the word *Christ,* would become real Christians.

You can find the path to unity as easily as you follow the boardwalk through a swamp. As soon as you step off the right path, you sink in the bog of separation, dispute, and evil.

True good is what is good for all.

Universal Love

A wise man from India said, "Just as a mother protects, raises, and pampers her only child, in this same way you should encourage and protect in yourself the most precious of your possessions, your ability to love others."

When we love others, and when we are loved, we feel good. This demonstrates that our true goodness is revealed only in love.

If you understand that love is the most important thing in the world, then when you meet someone, you should care not about their usefulness to you but how you can help them. If you do this, you accomplish a lot more than when you think only of yourself.

Why do I believe in the law of love and follow it? What will come of it? I don't know. But I do know that the more I follow the law, the better it is for me and for others.

Sin

 As time passes, you should try to eliminate your mistakes. If you fail to see your life as liberating, and to rid yourself of the errors of your past, then you're making the biggest mistake of all.

There is no one without sin, no one who has not made mistakes. Ridding yourself of your sins should be the chief purpose of your life.

It can be hard to think about your sins, but what a great joy it is to be free of them. If there were no darkness, we would not rejoice in sunrise.

If you have to be right, then you cannot confront your sins. When others reveal your mistakes and sins to you, the worst possible response is anger, which becomes just one more sin.

Desire and Passion

 A person cannot truly be virtuous. Therefore, try to abstain from lust, bad language, gluttony, and drunkenness. The more balanced the life you lead, the more joyful it will become.

A moth flies into a bonfire's light without knowing the fire will burn its wings. A fish swallows the bait without realizing it may result in death. We know our sexual appetites can ruin us, yet nevertheless we give ourselves over to them.

There is hardly a subject more confusing than sexual relationships. Therefore, the best would be for people to discuss it with sincerity, out in the open.

Some look to marriage to satisfy their lust, but that doesn't stop them from feeling lustful.

Temptation

 "He eats simple fare, but he is a great man." This is a good proverb that we all should follow.

When you pursue bodily pleasures and live only to pamper them, then inevitably you lose the ability to feel pleasure.

When you could have walked for a while but instead drove, your legs began to weaken. In the same way, when we become used to luxuries and the trappings of wealth, we begin to forget simple living and lose our inner joy and peace and freedom.

Many among our contemporaries believe one has to serve one's body first. However, the wise men of the past have always affirmed that needing less is better.

Greed and Wealth

 Most great fortunes were achieved not by hard work but from crime.

To increase riches really means to increase love. Love is not only different from wealth but is its complete opposite. A person who lives by love can neither accumulate great wealth nor keep it if he already has it.

A poor man laughs more often and is more likely to be happy than a rich man.

When people live by the spirit, they don't need riches at all.

Earth is our common mother. It shelters us and feeds us from the instant we are born to the moment we return to it, to slumber eternally. But in spite of all this, people refer to it as a sellable good: "Land for sale and on the market." Land is not the property of one person, family, or generation, but belongs to the many generations who have lived and worked on it.

— THOMAS CARLYLE

Work and Idleness

 Do not stand at the door of a rich man asking for favors. You should never be afraid of hard work.

No matter how beautiful the garment given to you by a king, your own clothing is better. No matter how delicious the food of the rich, the bread from your own table tastes better.

A person lives two lives at the same time, material and spiritual, for each of which there are laws. The law of material life is work. The law of spiritual life is love. If you break the law of material life, that is, work, then inevitably you will break the law of spiritual life, that is, love.

When you are paid for your work by others, you never know what your labor truly costs. When I sit at court, play violin, and write books, I receive daily a hundred, even a thousand times more than a worker does for a hard day of physical labor.

I ask myself: Do I cost that much? Therefore, so as not to be in the wrong, try to work a lot and ask little for your work.

Anger and Hatred

 If you live a godly, spiritual life, you cannot be angry at others. God is love, and love cannot be angry. Thus your spirit, as part of the divine, cannot be angry as well.

Refrain from anger toward others, including animals. To be angry at animals is worse, since a man can at least understand the reason for your anger while an animal cannot.

The more you think of yourself as superior, the more anger you feel. A humble person is a kind person.

Contemplate revenge, and you make your wounds worse. They would heal faster if you made no effort to seek vengeance.

There is nowhere on earth, not the sky, the sea, or the mountaintops, where a person can be rid of evil if he lets it into his heart. You need to remember this.   — INDIAN PROVERB

Pride

 If someone is going about life in the wrong way, rather than improve his life he will try to find justifications for it — for example, that he is better than others. From this it appears that a person living a bad life must be filled with self-pride.

You cannot have pride without stupidity. However, you can have stupidity without pride.

We all are given a great gift, the gift of our very life, with all its joys and pleasures. Yet we often say that we are not happy.

Nothing results in bad deeds and actions more than belonging to a group of people, a club or society, who think they are better than others. The most astonishing fact is that belonging to such a closed society is considered by some to be a virtue.

Vanity and Fame

 Throughout history, people have mocked those who kept silent. They have also mocked those who spoke out. People gossip about and mock everyone on this earth. There is no one who is blameless and no one who was only praised. Therefore, pay no attention to blame or praise.

Heaven is angry at us for our sins, and the world is angry at us for our virtues.

As soon as you come down from the heights where you live for your spirit, you immediately dive into the world of people's petty opinions, judgments, and fame.

Be more concerned with the quality of your friends than with their number.

It happens sometimes that after performing a great service to others, you are disappointed. This is because you served not for God's sake, but for fame and vanity.

Judgment and Punishment

Some people say that evil should be punished by another evil, violence by more violence. Yet this is not true. People act this way out of revenge, not to punish evil. You cannot cure evil by practicing evil.

If I can force others to do what I think is good, then someone can force me to do what he thinks is good, even if we have opposing views on the subject.

The desire to punish, to pay back, to extract revenge — this desire is not proper to humans but a part of our animal side. Therefore, we should free ourselves from this feeling and not justify it.

Our life would be beautiful if we could eliminate the things that destroy our happiness. The false idea that punishment is good destroys our happiness, and thus, our good life.

True kindness in not only a virtue but also a weapon, a weapon more powerful than violence.

Violence and War

 We should respect others, and not tell them what to do. People must have dignity.

Why do people have an intellect if it's true that they can be governed only by violence?

How strange! We become angry at the evil around us, which we cannot change, yet we do nothing to conquer the evil inside us, which we can.

It makes sense that cows, horses, and sheep are guarded by men. Men know better than these animals how to feed and take care of them. But why do some people tell others what to do? All people are intelligent beings, and they can be guided only by something superior to them, that is, by spirit.

Faith

What is prayer? It is appealing to the higher state of your spirit and trying to remind yourself that you are a spiritual being. When you talk to another person, it is a mystery, as if you are talking to God. I try to remember this every time I talk to people.

True prayer occurs when we ignore worldly things, connect to the divine within us, and so communicate with God. When we think of ourselves as good servants and give Him our whole being — our spirit, our actions, and our decisions — this is true prayer.

In religion, you have to separate what was taught by Jesus from who Jesus is. Then you will know the good news that comes from love.

The lesson of love cannot support its opposite. It cannot be used to justify war and capital punishment.

Faith

 As soon as you understand the teachings of Christ in their true sense, you will see the lies of our education.

To lie to another is bad. But worst of all is to lie to yourself, especially in the area of faith.

Every teaching of faith considered to be final and true should be verified by your intellect.

Every lie is poison; there are no harmless lies. Only the truth is safe. Only truth is so firm that I can rely on it. Only truth gives me consolation — it is the one unbreakable diamond.

This is what real faith is: it is not to be found in rituals or formal sacrifices but in the unification of the people.

False Science

 Everyone's primary task is to become a better and better person. Only those sciences are good that assist us in this goal.

Knowledge is limitless. Therefore, we cannot say that a person who knows a great deal knows more than another who knows very little.

Our younger generations are being taught numerous complicated subjects, such as celestial mechanics or astronomy, the development of our planet over millions of years, or the evolution of the species, and so on. Yet they are not taught the answer to the most necessary question — what is the purpose of our life?

Real knowledge is acquired not by memory, but through intellectual effort.

We can start to understand the world when we forget what we were taught.

Effort

 Here on earth, there is no peace, nor should there be. Life is a striving toward an unobtainable goal, and as such, there can be no peace or pause. I may not know exactly what the purpose of our life is, but achieving it, moving toward it, can be done only with effort.

All of our history supports this indisputable truth: God cannot be understood by logical reasoning but only by submission. First, we have to feel in our hearts what we are and what we should be. Second, we have to make an effort to get to where we should go. We are free to make a choice — to go on living in sin or put an end to it.

Our greatest achievements have been the products of quiet inner work with respect to the soul and not products of violent, rushed efforts. Similarly, a door to a palace is opened quietly only when pulled gently, not pushed with great force.

Self-Sacrifice

 Denying yourself does not mean to deny living. To the contrary, you increase your true, spiritual life by denying the bodily life of your flesh.

Real self-sacrifice occurs only when a person denies animal life for divine spiritual life. The world means nothing if you live in God.

In the same way that a plant cannot live without sunlight, people cannot live without love.

There is no greater love than when you readily give your love to your friends. Real life is always a sacrifice.

All good things are accomplished when a person forgets about himself. The world exists only because people act in this way.

Humility and Modesty

 When people scold you, be joyful. When they praise you, be sad.

There is no quality — such as beauty, power, wealth, education, and even kindness — that without humility would not disappear or turn into its opposite.

Remember that good deeds are acts of God and can be performed and achieved without you. And even if you get to participate slightly in a good deed, it is as a special blessing and not because of any merit of your own.

For the humble and meek, all is easy, light, and good. We all know this. But when we start to live according to this premise, we see that our yoke is not easy and our burden is not light. What does this mean? Either the premise is not true, or we are not meek and humble enough.

Truth

 One of the most important tasks to accomplish in your life is to fulfill the intellectual potential given to you by God.

Our mind and our intellect are two different things. We understand everyday life with our mind. We comprehend our soul and God with our intellect.

Truth is the beginning and the end of our existence. Truth does not exist by itself but is created by love. Truth is love.

It is good to reveal the lies of others but even better to reveal your own lies to yourself. You should indulge in this pleasure more often.

Misunderstandings between good and honest people do happen, mostly because they underestimate their intellect.

Temptation

A good groom doesn't throw away the reins if the horses don't stop at once. Instead he pulls until the horses come to a halt. In the same way, you should constantly fight your bad habits and cravings. In doing so, you will defeat them, and they won't prevail over you.

Do not crave something so much that you cannot stand it. Anyone has the power to break any bad habit.

Every man reminds me of a working horse in harness, ready to plow the field. You have to work in this life regardless of whether you want to or not, but some people concentrate on materialistic work and some on spiritual growth.

A person who commits physical sins, such as gluttony, drunkenness, lust, or anger, can see them and eliminate them if he chooses. The person who commits moral sin, such as pride or excessive wealth, cannot always percieve these sins and temptations with his eyes.

Anger and Hatred

 Love between people is the best thing in the world. Be careful not to destroy this love with your words.

The beginning of a quarrel is like water trying to break through a dam. When the dam is broken, you cannot stop the current. And each quarrel begins with words.　　— THE TALMUD

An argument convinces no one, but rather divides people and makes them angry.

We almost always find in ourselves the same sin we blame in others.

If two people are hostile to each other, they are both at fault. If just one of them ceased to be hostile, the disagreement would quickly disappear.

Thoughts

Wisdom is precious, both our own and the wise thoughts uttered by others. These wise thoughts can help you more than anything else to achieve your goal.

When we hear a new thought and think it good, it often seems that we have known it always. All great truths already exist deep in your soul.

There are two kind of people: those who think first, then speak and act, and those who speak and act first, then think.

It is good to pray in solitude, as Christ taught us. However, we can also pray together with other people. Group prayer is just as important. When we meet with others, we should remember that the same spirit resides in all of us.

Changes in our lives start with the changes in our thoughts. Changes in how we think are much more important than the efforts we make to change our lives.

There Is No Evil

I pray to God to relieve the suffering that is troubling me. However, this suffering was sent to me by God so that I could overcome evil. A master whips his cattle to drive them out of a burning barn, to save them, but the cattle pray not to be whipped.

Small problems can make us lose our balance. Big problems, to the contrary, can bring us back to real life, our spiritual life.

People need pain and illnesses; our sufferings help us understand our blessings. If it weren't for our suffering, pain, and failures, we would have nothing to compare to our joy, happiness, and success.

Look for the opportunities to further your spiritual growth; then the bitter part of suffering will disappear.

Living in the Present

 We say that time goes by, but this is not true. Like a boat, it is we who are moving, not time. When we go down the river in a boat, it just seems to us that the riverbanks are moving, and not the boat.

Life is too short. There is not enough time in our brief lives to bring enough joy to our loved ones. Therefore, let us make haste to show acts of kindness.

The concept of life seems clear and simple at first. "I love with my body, therefore life is in my body." But where exactly in your body do you look for it? Life is not in your nails, your hair, your arms, or your legs — or in your very blood. Then you start looking at your life in time. I lived first twenty years, then thirty, forty, fifty, and sixty years. But I know I slept away a third of that. Did I live then? When I was in my mother's womb, did I live then? Therefore, if life cannot be measured in space or found in time, it exists outside of space and time, that is, in the spirit.

Death

 There is nothing terrible about death, except for what we have created to scare ourselves.

Remember, you do not abide but rather pass through this life. You are not in a house but on a train that takes you to death. Remember, only your body will die, and only the spirit is truly alive.

Look at a group of prisoners in shackles. They are all sentenced to death. Some are executed, while others watch. Those who survive see all this and become terrified. This is the life of men who do not understand the meaning of life.

Spiritual life cannot be measured by material measurements.

Evil and pain make me suffer, but death liberates me. How then can I not consider it good?

After Death

 People ask, "What will happen after death?" Give yourself into the hands of the Divine Creator, for you know He is all love and goodness. You can thus be assured that everything will be good.

The more spiritual our life becomes, the more we believe in eternity. The veil is removed from the future, the darkness disperses, and we feel we are eternal.

I do not believe in any of the existing religions, but I have deep and profound thoughts about the law of life. I have looked at the history of thought, at the history of mankind, then inside my inner self, and I came to the conclusion that there is no death. There can be only one eternal life, and the eternal moving toward perfection is the law of life.

Faith

 An unbeliever is not someone who doesn't believe what he has been taught but someone who says he believes when he doesn't.

Every religion has its answer to the question: "How can I live my life — not for humanity but for the force that brought me into this world?"

For most of mankind, religion is a tradition, or more precisely, tradition is religion. The first step to moral perfection — as strange as it may seem — is to liberate yourself from the religion you grew up with. As far as I know, no one has come to spiritual development along any other path than this. — HENRY DAVID THOREAU

Hesitations do not destroy but strengthen faith.

True religion is a religion of the intellect; it does not oppose the intellect.

Soul

 Our conscience is the voice of the spirit that lives in us all.

When you suffer, look for consolation within. Don't seek it in books or temples. Only God, who lives in you, will help you.

A man is like a flightless bird that can only run on the ground. When this bird suddenly understands there is something inside it that can lift it up, it finds freedom and goodness. This something above our bodily life is our understanding of the spirit within us, which is the essence of Christ's teaching.

We have built airplanes — to fly where? We have constructed railways and highways — to travel where? We have telephones — to talk about what? Stop and think for a moment: Why do we live here? Stop, think about your inner self, your spirit, and try to save yourself. Then, you will save the world.

One Soul in All

 If you hate your brother, you first hate yourself.

It is not enough to say that each person has a s-i-m-i-l-a-r spirit living inside of him, it is the s-a-m-e spirit that lives in us all, myself included.

You always feel good after doing a good deed. Every good act done for others proves that the true "me" is not found in yourself alone but in every living being.

Only those who recognize the same God in every person can embrace God in themselves.

Remember, the same spirit lives in everyone. It lives in you, in me, and in others. Thus, you should not only love others but treat them as holy, because you are addressing their spirit, which is the same as your own.

God

 God does not exist only for those who have found Him. Seek God — and He will reveal Himself to you.

God loves solitude. He will enter your heart only when He alone is around you, and when you are thinking only about Him.

You can feel God inside you; it is possible and not difficult to do. However, understanding God is not possible, nor is it necessary.

Only those who follow the law of God will get to know God better. You can come closer to God only though good deeds and love.

When a person loudly cries, "Oh, God is here," he has not found God. Those who find God keep silent. — RAMAKRISHNA

Unification in Spirit

You believe you want good only for yourself only because of your limitations. But this is just how it seems. The desire to do what is good is the voice of God living within you, and God desires goodness for all.

The purpose of life is to set your spirit free from your body, and unite with other spirits and God. Life is pleasant when you grasp this concept.

Living for others and not yourself elevates your life from your body to your spirit, so you can reach for the heights, where there is no time, death, or evil.

You only truly become free when you unite with the whole world.

Universal Love

 Try to love all people. Get into the habit of loving, and you will see how your life will fill with more joy and happiness.

If you live well, it won't matter whether people blame or praise you, or even if they cease to love you. But whether you want it or not, good and kind people will love you, and evil people will no longer hate or harm you.

Oh God, give me the ability to love You, and give me love for the ones You love.

— MUHAMMAD

I know only one greatest good in the world — when you are loved. But you cannot reach it by seeking how to be loved. The only way to achieve this is to follow the law of life, the will of God, and strive for spiritual perfection.

Sin

It is a mistake to think you can rid yourself of your sins through the forgiveness of others. No, you can be rid of your sins only by understanding them and making a conscious effort to eliminate them, not by being forgiven.

Every mistake, every sin, you commit binds you. First it binds you as if you were caught in a spider's web. If you repeat the sin, it becomes a small rope, then a bigger one. If you continue to repeat it, it becomes an iron chain.

Sin comes to you first as a onetime visitor, turns into a frequent guest, and finally becomes the master of the house.

If there were no spirit in your body, there would be no life. The body binds the spirit; the spirit is always trying free itself from the body. This is what life is all about.

Desire and Passion

God's divine spirit lives in every man or woman. It is a sin to look at the bearer of God's spirit as a source for your bodily pleasures. Therefore, every woman to a man is first his sister, and every man to a woman is first her brother.

You cannot imagine a saint as a married man. The closer someone is to the holy life, the more chaste he becomes.

The Bible says a husband and his wife are not two separate beings but one. This is very true. The sexual union of these two leads to a new life, and unites them in a mysterious way.

The spiritual, brotherly love between a man and a woman can be stronger than any sexual attraction between them.

Temptation

 Just as smoke drives bees from their hive, drinking and overeating drive the best spiritual power out of a person.

If you constantly overeat, it is hard not to be lazy. If you drink too much, it is hard to be celibate.

A person goes outside with a lantern into the darkness of night and has difficulty finding his way. When he gets tired, he blows his lantern out, heading in any direction, no longer caring where he is going. The same happens to us when we put out the light of our intellect by smoking and drinking, and lose our true path, our direction in life.

We should eat to live, not live to eat.

Greed and Wealth

 Just as wearing heavy clothes slows your body down, riches weigh down your soul.

If a poor person envies a rich man, he is no better than the rich man.

Great wealth achieved with so much effort and sin has only one true value: the pleasure you experience when you get rid of it.

If you take people's money, goods, or cattle, your theft ends when you leave, for all these things can be replaced. When you take away people's land and destroy their connection to the earth, your robbery lasts forever, robbing every generation, every year, and every day.

— HENRY GEORGE

Simplicity in language, lifestyle, and tradition gives power to a nation. Luxury and sophistication lead to the weakness and death of a nation.

131

Work and Idleness

 Most of us have to work, and work hard all the time. The difference lies in what you do.

Having a good rest after a day of hard work is one of the best and purest joys in the world.

No one has counted the millions of hours and thousands of lives given for the entertainment of the rich. This is a sad fact that does not amuse me.

When you use any material object, remember that it is the concentration of human labor. If you break it, damage it, or throw it away, you are showing little respect for people's work.

Hell hides behind pleasure, paradise hides behind work and trouble. — MUHAMMAD

Judgment and Punishment

 I know myself enough to know that I do not want to commit evil deeds. If I have ever committed one, it was circumstantial. Most people are like me in that, if they commit an evil deed, it happens due to circumstances. So why then do I blame others?

Can you blame a sick person for his appearance? He is not to blame if you are disgusted by his sores. In the same way, do not treat other people's vices with disgust, but be patient and use your intellect.

You can clearly see the fact that you have lost your purse, so why don't you weep over the most precious things you have lost, your intellect and kindness?

It often happens that we are filled with sin but cannot stand the sin we see in others.

Pride

 There are many punishments for the proud, the most difficult being that no matter how many virtues they have, they are unloved.

You are right to think no one is superior to you, but you are mistaken if you think at least one person is inferior to you.

The proud are so busy teaching others, they have no time to think about themselves, as they feel they are good enough already. The more they teach others, the lower they fall.

Learn from the water in the depths of the sea and in mountain crevasses: shallow creeks make a lot of noise, but the deep sea is silent and hardly moving.

People often consider others to be inferior or superior to themselves. They should remember that the same spirit lives in all.

Vanity and Fame

When children play, they separate into competing teams but know as soon as the game is over that they are all friends again. However, when adults are divided into classes, social groups, and nations, they often remain in these groups for the rest of their lives.

If you worry too much about being praised, it becomes difficult to act. Some will praise you for one thing, while others will praise you for something else. Only you can decide what to do in your life, and knowing this will make your life a lot easier.

It is difficult to break from accepted traditions, but with every step you take to become better, you are forced to break some old, generally accepted rules, conventions, and opinions.

I feel ashamed that I have not lived according to my conscience and have followed the stupid rules, habits, and traditions of others.

Judgment and Punishment

People don't believe they should return good for evil, simply because they have been taught the opposite since childhood.

Forgiving others doesn't just mean saying "I forgive" but also removing all reproach from your heart. To do this, remember your sins.

The essence of all religious teachings — including Christianity — is love. The Christian teaching is unique in many ways, especially because it says that all forms of violence are unacceptable to love.

Every time violence is used, try to apply logical reasoning against it. You may lose in the worldly sense, but you will gain a great deal in the spiritual.

Violence and War

The cruelty of all coups and revolutions in history can be explained by the cruelty of the previous rulers. If people were not taught violence early on, they would not have applied it.

You were created neither to force nor to obey. People are spoiled by both. Stupidity or pride causes it — but there is no human dignity in either.

Teach your heart, and do not learn from it.
— BUDDHIST PROVERB

The capital punishment that exists in some countries today is the obvious proof that the foundation of our society is foreign to Christianity.

The purpose of man is to serve God and all people, not serve some and do evil to others.

Faith

Every religion says it is the one true faith, that all other faiths and religions are false. This in itself is enough to see that no single religion is the true one.

When people blindly believe any teaching as the law of God, they do not use their God-given ability to think, through which they can truly understand God's law.

Faith teaches us both what to do and how to understand this life. For thousands of years, people did not know how to properly understand the law of God. Some people believe all ancient things are good, but this is not so, and to believe it is a great mistake.

The safety and well-being of a society depend on the morality of its members, and morality is based on religion.

Prayer

You cannot get to know God by listening to stories about Him. You get to know Him only by following His law, which is written in the heart of every person.

A little boy once went to bed and asked his nurse to pray for him and continue to play with his dolls while he slept. People have the same childish attitude toward God. They believe they can live bad lives, go to bed, and be prayed for by someone who will continue to play the game for them.

A person can live without prayer only when his sins are guiding him or when he is a saint. One necessary condition for a good life is when those who resist their passions, prejudices, and lies in this world seek a higher understanding of the meaning of love.

False Science

 As long as people have been living in this world, they have had teachers to tell them what is most important.

There are an unlimited number of sciences, but without the knowledge of what is good and your purpose in this life, you cannot make the right choice.

Nowadays, there is a huge amount of knowledge worth our study. Yet over time our abilities grow too weak, and our life is too short, to learn even the smallest, most necessary part of this knowledge.

If we could think independently, we could do without a lot of unnecessary reading. It is harmful to read too much. The greatest thinkers I've met among scholars were those who read the least.

If you read bad books, you cannot read too few; if you read good books, you cannot read too many. Bad books are like moral poison.

Effort

 Remember that freeing yourself from sin or prejudice is the most important thing you can do — more important than fame, wealth, and education.

Unclear things must be clarified. Difficult things should be dealt with using all of your energy, without giving in.

Life in this world is not changed by external rules and regulations but by the inner striving of every individual.

It can be hard not to do something but even harder not to do something you know is evil or wrong.

Moral action is measured not by how important it is, but how much effort you put into it.

Self-Sacrifice

 You can truly love only God, and you can truly despise only yourself.

Every person already has the understanding of life.

It is only by denying his individuality that a person can become a true person. You can understand this limitless life only by understanding your own life through the lives of others.

People think self-denial violates freedom, but our own intimate passions are the worst dictators. As soon as you are able to deny them, you gain your true freedom.

Self-denial is a part of human nature, as seen in the fact that sacrificing for a good cause brings you joy. However, it never fully satisfies you, for you always can do more.

Humility and Modesty

The entranceway to the Temple of Goodness and Knowledge is found low to the ground. Only the humble will bow down to enter it. However, once inside the temple, you will find immense space and freedom, and love for all people. This temple is our life; the entrance is the teaching of wisdom. And wisdom is revealed to the humble.

A person who stands on his toes cannot manage it for very long. A person who is satisfied with himself cannot be famous. A person who is proud cannot be superior.

Be careful of thinking yourself better than others, that you have virtues other people don't. No matter how good your virtues, they are worthless if you think too highly of them.

If you do something good for your neighbor, forget about it. If you do something bad, try not to forget. Remind yourself of it so you can improve yourself.

Truth

 Lies move God away from us all. Thus, there is nothing better than truth and the defeat of lies.

The purpose of intelligence is to eliminate lies and establish the truth. However, intelligence, under the sway of passion, becomes the lies' defender. It becomes not only perverted but ill, losing its ability to distinguish truth from lies, good from bad. Every kind of lie or misconception, no matter where it is found, should be dealt with, as there are no harmless or useful lies.

Always tell the truth, no matter how bitter and unpleasant it may be to other people.

Your conscience is your greatest asset. Your conscience is the quality that in the thick of everyday things helps you see the real truth.

There Is No Evil

We feel illness as an affliction, a burden, but illness is an important part of life. It shows us that our bodies live a temporary, not an eternal life.

As soon as a new and higher ideal is set before mankind, all previous ideals dim by comparison, like stars fading in the rays of the rising sun. People then cannot help but accept this new ideal and strive toward it.

To help yourself not do evil deeds, first try to avoid evil conversation. Even more important is to rid yourself of all evil thoughts.

As soon as you learn to avoid evil thoughts, you will learn to avoid evil deeds.

Most people we consider evil are simply in a bad mood and cannot control their temper.

Words

 We know we need to treat a loaded rifle with care. But we don't like to think that we need to treat what we say with the same caution.

A word can kill or, in some cases, cause even worse harm than death.

Those who speak too much, do little. A wise person is always aware that his words can be louder than his deeds, and therefore keeps silent for a long time before he speaks. He speaks only for the necessity of others.

If you have the time to think before you start talking, then consider whether it is worth speaking at all, or whether you may harm someone with what you are going to say.

Silence is the best response to a stupid man. Any bad word or criticism bounces back to you. Adding another offense to the first is the same as throwing wood on the fire.

Thoughts

A cow, horse, or any other animal cannot leave a corral if the gate opens by pulling toward the inside. They would die from hunger, because they are unable to fathom the gate. Only humans understand that you sometimes have to do what you don't like in order to reach your goal. Humans have intelligence, our most precious and important ability, and we should nurture and encourage it to grow.

Our established way of thinking interprets everything we encounter in our lives. If these preconceived notions are false, they taint the most exalted truth. We carry our old thoughts and views on life as a snail carries its house on its back wherever it goes.

Just as a farmer separates his best seeds from the bad, and nurtures and takes care of them, so a clever person does with his thoughts. He gets rid of the bad ones, keeps the best ones, and cares for them.

There Is No Evil

It is only when you live for your body alone that your suffering seems evil to you. If you think the purpose of your life is to improve your inner self, then you will come to understand that suffering is good for you; for without it, there can be no spiritual improvement.

Accept each misfortune that befalls you with the same attitude as a sick man taking his medicine. We know that medicine can be bitter and disgusting to the taste, but we feel better when we take it. In the same way, rejoice over your hardship and trouble, because they are good for your soul.

You suffer only when you separate yourself from the world, believe you are innocent of your sins, and fail to connect your suffering with your spiritual growth.

If you are afraid of something, know that the reason for your fear is found not without, but within you.

Living in the Present

You torture yourself with your past, and in doing so spoil your future because you are not busy enough in the present. The past is over, the future does not yet exist, there is only the present.

Good people quickly forget the acts of kindness they have done. They are so busy with what they are doing in the present that they do not think about what they have done in the past.

The older you are, the faster time goes by, and the less meaning it holds for you. "What will happen?" means less than "What happens now?"

The notions of space and time demonstrably prove the weakness of our intellect. We cannot imagine anything beyond them, but this does not make sense, for it contradicts logic. Time should indicate limits in the sequencing of events; space, the limits in the locations of objects. Both time and space, however, have no limits.

Death

 You should live both in eternity and in the present. Work as if you will live forever, and treat others as if you may die tonight.

Everything in this life is simple, interconnected, and can be explained. Everything, except for death, and so people try not to think about it. This is a mistake. We should simply look at life as a part of something mysterious and incomprehensible, and death as something simple, clear, and easily understood.

The most important thing for our spiritual life is to understand that we are not standing still in one place but constantly moving somewhere at great speed.

In this life, we are passengers on a huge ship. The captain has a secret list, which says who shall leave the ship and when. While on the ship, we need to flow with the law of life and live in peace, love, and harmony with all our friends during the time we are given.

After Death

People ask what happens to us after we die. We don't know and cannot know. But one thing is true. If we are to go somewhere, we must have come from somewhere. We will return from whence we came.

Time obscures death. When you live in time, you cannot imagine how it could stop. Death is the end of time.

Do not fear death. To the contrary, death should be joyful to the person who has lived a truthful life. — MARCUS AURELIUS

Life is beautiful. When we say this life is bad, it is often in comparing it to the afterlife, about which we know nothing.

Happiness

Remember that if a person is unhappy, only he is to blame, for God created us all to be happy. People are unhappy because they desire what they cannot have. When they are happy, they are content with what they have.

If you are not happy with your life, you can change it in two ways: either improve the conditions in which you live, or improve your inner spiritual state. The first is not always possible, but the second is.

You want to live in paradise, where there is no suffering or animosity? Then liberate your heart, set it free and fill it with love. There you will find the heaven you desire.

We should thank God for making all good things easy and all that hinders goodness difficult.

Do not search for pleasure. Rather, be ready to find pleasure in anything you do.

— JOHN RUSKIN

Faith

 True faith is not knowing the days of fasting, the church's schedule, or what prayers to read — but daily living a good life, being kind to your neighbor, treating him or her as you want to be treated. This is true faith.

All the true and wise men of every nation teach this: Do not be afraid to purge your faith of all unnecessary things — physical, material, and visible. The better you cleanse your spiritual core, the better you understand the law of life.

You do not need anything to complete the task of living other than doing what is good and acting accordingly.

Society cannot live a kind and intelligent life without religion. You can force but not convince people without religion.

Soul

 Everyone lives by the spirit, but not everyone knows it. If a person is unaware of this, he has everything to fear. As soon as you believe your life is in your spirit, there is nothing to fear, for no one can harm your spirit.

In the most important questions of your life, you are always alone. No one other than you can understand your true history, your life story, as it develops. The essence of true life is your attitude, during the different stages of your life, toward your spiritual self, and your ability to follow that voice living inside you.

No matter where you go, your thoughts always go with you, along with your inner spirit, the concentration of your life, freedom, and power.

To grasp the true meaning of things, you need to shift your gaze from the visible to the invisible, from the material to the spiritual. To see the true light as it is, you yourself need to become this true light.

One Soul in All

 Your happiness is found in service to your loved ones and your neighbors. You will find this happiness because, when you serve others, you become one with the spirit living in us all.

Rid yourself of everything that prevents you from connecting with all living creatures. Try to strengthen this connection as much as you can.

A branch cut at its base is cut from the whole tree as well. In the same fashion, a man who quarrels with others is cut away from mankind. The difference lies in the fact that a branch is cut away by someone else's hand, whereas a quarrelsome man cuts himself off from others by his evil deeds or his anger.

Often, a person cannot understand that the same spirit is in him, in others, and in God. Without this, how can you understand your life?

— KRISHNA

God

 When you have difficulties, have lost your connection with God, or have doubts about God's existence, you do better to stop thinking about God. Instead, think only about His law of life, and how to fulfill it by loving everyone. Only then will you find God.

While a person may not see that he breathes air, when there is not enough air to breathe he will know something is missing that he cannot live without. The same happens to a person who has lost his faith in God. He suffers without knowing why.

I cannot understand God, but I know Him, I know how to find Him, and of all my knowledge this is the most important and the most real.

The essence of God cannot be captured with words. God is beyond words.

— ANGELUS SILESIUS

Unification in Spirit

 God lives in each and every one of us. As soon as the spirit awakens in you, it wants to unite with God and with others.

While a person can live separately from others, spiritually he cannot live on his own. He wants to be united with others, and with the Source of all.

The more you live for your body, the less you communicate and unite with others.

There is no peace for those who live only a material life or those who live only a spiritual life. You will find peace when you live both your spiritual and physical lives among others.

Do not concern yourself whether others love you or not. Love, and you will be loved by others.

Universal Love

 When we love others, we feel good at that moment. We are not afraid of anything and do not want anything else. Why does this happen? Simply put, because love is God. When we love others, we unite with God, and with everything else living in this world. What can we want, or fear, if we are united with God and the whole world?

Flower petals fall when the tree's fruit starts to grow. All your weaknesses fall away in the same fashion, when your spirit begins to grow inside of you.

Love everyone: the poor in spirit, the rich and spoiled, the lost, the proud, as well as the physically disabled. Do not argue, get angry, or blame them. If you can, try to help them in any way, for being spiritually crippled can be even worse than being physically crippled.

Love others not for your personal benefit but because love brings you happiness.

Sin

 You cannot live completely without sin, but you can get rid of some sins and live with fewer. This process of ridding yourself of sin, mistakes, and prejudices is the true life, and the true good for everyone.

People can hear two opposing voices inside themselves. One voice tells you to live only for yourself; the other says to give to those in need. One voice says repay evil with evil; the other, forgive. The first voice says to listen to others; the second voice, listen to your inner spirit. You make the right choice when you listen to your second voice, your true inner voice.

If you become obsessed by a passion, remember this passion is not a part of your spirit and you can free yourself from it. As a rule, this passion is an obstacle to getting in touch with your inner spirit. When you rid yourself of it, you will be reunited with your inner self.

Temptation

 We should learn from animals how to treat our bodies. As soon as an animal receives what it needs for its body, it calms down. However, humans never have enough to satisfy their hunger. We invent ever more sophisticated drink and food in our attempt to do so.

The ancient Greek wise man, Pythagoras, did not eat meat. When another Greek writer, Plutarch, was asked why Pythagoras went without it, he responded that he was not surprised by this fact but rather by the fact that so many, already having so much food with seeds, nuts, fruits, and vegetables, would venture to catch, kill, and eat animals.

It is difficult to imagine the positive, wholesome changes that can happen in your life if you stop poisoning it with wine, vodka, tobacco, and drugs.

The less you wish for, the happier you will be. This is an old truth, but not one accepted and understood by everybody.

Desire and Passion

 The sexual feelings in both men and animals are given for a great cause, to continue your family line. It is wrong to think that these sexual feelings were given only for pleasure.

As with everything in life, you should not have too many tasks in marriage. There should be only one chief task to achieve — living a good life together and raising and educating your children.

You should think over your decision to marry many times before getting married. Joining your life to another sexually is one of the most important acts of your existence and can have far-reaching consequences, further than you can imagine. This can be the most important decision you ever make in your life.

What should a sexually pure young man and woman do in regard to the question of sex? What should be their guide? The answer is they should strive for celibacy before marriage, and if they get married, to remain pure in this regard.

Work and Idleness

 The noblest work is that of the farmer, who labors in the soil.

What is the best food? The food you have earned with your own hands. — MUHAMMAD

One of the greatest advantages of a working life, as compared to the lives of the idle, is the serious, solid, and positive thinking of working people when compared to the shallow thoughts and cheap conversation of the idle.

Some people think that doing laundry, cooking, and babysitting are exclusively women's work and not for men, even that it is shameful for men to do them. Yet what is truly a shame is when men sit idle or relax when a tired, weak, or pregnant woman is struggling to do all this hard work.

Greed and Wealth

 A rich man lives an uncomfortable life, as he is always afraid to lose his riches. The wealthier he is, the more worries he will have. A rich man can meet and be friends only with the rich, because he cannot be a real friend to the poor, for then the sin of his wealth will be too obvious.

The rich who give to charities are hypocrites, as the very money they give is often snatched from the hands of even poorer people.

Everywhere I look, I see the conspiracy of the rich, who, under the pretext of helping the poor, seek out any advantage and profit only for themselves. — SIR THOMAS MORE

A compassionate man is never rich. But a rich man has no compassion.
— CHINESE PROVERB

Poverty would disappear if everyone was seeking truth and the kingdom of God.

Anger and Hatred

When one person decides to harm another for everyone's sake, the hurt person may decide to repay the first with evil, and so people bring harm to each other while thinking they are acting in the best interest of all involved. This is exactly what is happening in the world today.

If only we could imagine ourselves in the place of others, we could eliminate our feelings of mutual hatred. If we mentally put others in our place, we could vanquish our pride.

The best way to fight someone's anger is to say, "Let's pity this person!" As rain is to a fire, so compassion is to anger.

There are people who like to be angry. They like to yell, interrupt, and lecture others. These people are unpleasant. We should also remember that they are very unhappy, for they do not know the joy of a good mood or happiness. Rather than be angry at them, we should pity them.

Pride

 The major purpose of your life is to improve your spirit. Yet a proud person thinks he is already good enough. Why improve, if you are good enough? This shows that pride is an especially bad vice, because it interferes with our major task — self-improvement.

If a person likes only himself, he will inevitably end up being proud. Pride is love only for one's self.

Without accepting the equality of man, there can be no true love.

We often judge other people. We call someone kind, another evil, the third stupid, the fourth smart, etc. We should not do this. A person flows like a river. Every day, he may be different. The stupid grow smart, the evil become kind, and so on. You can judge a man for his past, but he is already different in the present.

Humility and Modesty

 You can only serve one — God or yourself. If you serve God, you have to fight sin and temptation. If you serve yourself, you don't have to do this, but you will become just like everyone else.

The benefit of serving God, when compared to serving men, is that with men, you want to appear before others better than you really are. It is different with God. He knows all of us intimately. You cannot just pretend to be better but truly have to become better in His eyes.

A wise man is upset that he cannot always do the good things he wants to do and is not upset when people form wrong judgments about him.

Those who know that God lives within our souls are quiet and humble. They do not care about other people's judgments.

Judgment and Punishment

 Asking how many times you need to forgive is like asking a recovering alcoholic how many times he should refuse a drink while constantly being offered one. If I decided not to drink, I would decline, no matter how many times one was offered. The same steadfastness is necessary for forgiveness.

Punishment, as applied to education, not only does not improve children but does the opposite, for it teaches children cruelty.

If the good people on this planet wish to stop the cruelties, wars, and other crimes that darken the happiness of humanity, know that you cannot achieve this result with fighting, force, and revenge but only through nonviolent, peaceful means.

God especially loves those who forgive the abuser, especially if the abuser is at your mercy.

Violence and War

It is only the person with no faith in God who actually believes that some people can forcibly improve the lives of others. Those who try to improve others' lives through force cannot see the good from the evil.

No conditions or circumstances can be used as an excuse for killing others, especially on a mass scale. This is a deliberate and clear violation of the will of God expressed in many religions, yet there are still many countries that allow mass murder in the form of capital punishment.

If instead of saving the world, everyone tried to save themselves, they could achieve a great deal more toward the goal of improving the world in general.

A dreamer can often see the future in his dreams but doesn't want to wait for it to come. He wants to move it closer by force during his lifetime, even if these changes would naturally come about over thousands of years.

Effort

 "The good news of the kingdom of God is being preached, and everyone is forcing his way into it. The kingdom of God is within you." (Luke 16:16, 17:21). These two New Testament verses mean we must make an effort if we are to unite our souls with God and build the kingdom of heaven. This can only be achieved when we strive for it.

Some think that to be a truly religious person, for example, a real Christian, you need to perform heroic deeds. This is not true. You do not need to do anything unusual or extraordinary, just make a constant effort.

People receive joy not by possessing the truth but by making the effort to find the truth. The same thing can be said of virtue. What is important is the effort you make to move closer to it.

Taking slow, small steps forward without stopping is the best way if you want to understand truth and the meaning of life.

Faith

 Prayer reminds you who you are and what your purpose is in life. Think this over in solitude, when you are not distracted by anything else.

When you pray, pray only for yourself. Do not think you can please God with your prayer. You please God only when you follow His will.

The evil of this world stems from the fact that people do not believe in the eternal and universal law of life.

They say true believers make up a church. Do we have them, these true believers? If so, where are they?

Among our lies and misconceptions about faith, the cruelest is the one that says how to teach faith to children. When a child asks, "What is this world?" we answer not with what we think, but what other people thought, people who lived a hundred years ago. Instead of the spiritual food he needs, the child receives spiritual poison.

False Science

 There is no shame or harm in not knowing something. You should be ashamed and embarrassed when you pretend to know what you actually do not.

It is the quality, and not the quantity, of knowledge that is important. You can know a great deal and yet still not know the most important things.

Those who pose questions to our scholars can receive thousands of sophisticated answers. However, they will not get the answer to the most important questions: "Who am I?" and "How should I live my life?"

A publicly revealed lie is as important for the good of men as a clearly stated truth.

It is better not to read any books than to read many and believe them all. You can be a clever man without a single book, but if you believe all that is written in books, you can quickly become a fool.

Effort

 The person who puts his life into understanding the world and its purpose will never have desperate situations. He does not need a noisy society; he has enough inner work. There is only one worry — to be free of evil within himself and to live peacefully with other people and with God.

You can have a good life if you constantly think about it. You should develop the ability to always do good.

Seek truth, right up to your death. God will help you and stand by you.

The law of life is not always clear — not even to the wise. But if we make the effort, it can be understood. — CONFUCIUS

Self-Sacrifice

Your body conceals the God in you.

Try to see the good in others, not only in yourself. Try to blame only yourself, not others.

You cannot force yourself to love, but you can remove the obstacles to love.

Self-denial is necessary and joyful only if it is denying one's self for the purpose of fulfilling the will of God's spirit living within.

If you understand that you should live for the spirit but nevertheless follow your own interests, you look like the man who locked himself out of his house and lost the key.

Humility and Modesty

 Goodness in man is found in brotherly love and unity with all people. Our pride is the major obstacle to this unification. Only with humility can you treat others with brotherly love.

The more you are satisfied with yourself, the less you are satisfied with others. And to the contrary, the more dissatisfied you are with yourself, the happier you are with others, and the better life you will live.

A person who loves himself has little competition. — GEORGE C. LICHTENBERG

When you are friendly, humble, and polite, God will come to you as naturally as the water flowing down into the valley.

— CHINESE PROVERB

Truth

 If certain people tell you not to seek the truth in everything you do, do not heed them, for they are your enemies. They tell you this because they don't live their lives according to truth and want others to do the same.

People who are not living according to truth find many different explanations for why their lives aren't bad but good.

The more complicated the life around you, the more you need your intelligence to find the solutions.

Truth will be your light. Truth will be your shelter. Seek support only in truth.

— BUDDHIST PROVERB

Truth is brief. Lies speak with many words.

Words

 Be in control of yourself if you want others to treat you as you want to be treated.

Neither praise nor boast about yourself. Never argue with others.

How important is moderation in words? You can see how important it is when you tell the truth when you're irritated, and you cannot convince anyone. Speak the truth with kindness, and everyone, even stupid people, will understand it.

It is good to agree with your friend to stop as soon as either of you starts accusing the other. If you don't have such a friend, make this agreement with yourself.

When after a lengthy conversation you try to remember what was said, you will be astonished at how many empty and unnecessary words were spoken.

Thoughts

Do not think only special people can be wise. Wisdom is a common quality, and everyone can have it. Wisdom is the knowledge of what is good in this life, and following it.

Wisdom comes in two ways: first, through spiritual growth achieved in solitude, and second, while communicating and discussing with others.

At the summit of your conscious life, you are lonely. Solitude can be difficult for an unwise man. The unwise try to distract themselves, and move to the lower levels of their spiritual life. The truly wise person keeps himself at this summit of inner solitude, while communicating with God in prayer.

A fruitful prayer re-creates in your conscious memory the highest understanding of the meaning of life as revealed to you during the best moments of your life.

There Is No Evil

 If we believe that our purpose in life is to improve ourselves, then all we consider evil cannot be an obstacle for us along this path.

The old proverb that "God gives suffering to those he loves" is a good one, for suffering liberates you from evil.

It is pitiful to watch the sufferings of an animal, a child, or a man. A clever person will either diminish or extinguish his suffering, by thinking of it as an important but temporary step, to be followed by joy or respite. After a period of hard work, there will be rest. If you are sick, you will get better. If you are hungry, you will taste food again. Every instance of suffering is followed by pleasure.

You get no closer to God than during times of misfortune and trouble. Try to take advantage of such times, as they will bring you good.

Living in the Present

 We understand that our willpower is free, that we are free and can do whatever we want. However, we should agree that if this is true, then our understanding of the law of reason, cause, and consequence is wrong. If this law were true, our willpower would not be free, and we would be bound by events that happened to us in the past.

There is no space or time in the spiritual world. Our thoughts and emotions are what is truly important.

You can fight your bad habits only today, not tomorrow. — CONFUCIUS

The free, divine energy of life is manifested only in the present. Therefore, the acts that take place in the present have divine qualities. Be clever and kind in the present.

179

Death

 Try to live your life in such a way that you are not afraid of death.

How can I be afraid of death, if I am used to dying each and every day when I go to bed and sleep, and then I have a better day on the morrow?

Socrates said of death that it is the same state we experienced before birth. We all know that there is nothing scary or bad in it. On the other hand, if death is a passage to a better life, as many people think, then death is not evil but good.

If you agree that life is spirit and not in your body, then there is no death, only the liberation of your spirit from your body.

After Death

Life reminds me of a caterpillar turning into a butterfly. Caterpillars cannot fly. First they are born, and then they change into cocoons. We will be butterflies in our future life.

People say the only good reality is where our personalities can be eternal. But my personality is the most disgusting thing in the world.

A child cries when he is born; a dying man is sorrowful when he dies. But they should both rejoice, as this is the most important moment for each of them. For the child, it is coming from the other side to here; for a dying man, it is crossing from here to the other side.

Can we not understand what our life will be like after death? Just as nothing bad happened to us before birth, nothing bad will happen to us after death.

Happiness

There are two kinds of people. The first group reminds me of stubborn animals pulled by their master to the barn where they have shelter and food. The animals resist the master, who wants what is good for them, but sooner or later they all go to the same place. The second group reminds me of animals who follow their master's will and freely go to the barn, as they know their master wants what is good for them.

In the long run, the complexity of our lives leads to an increase of love and, therefore, an increase of good as well.

Remember that the world did not come into existence by itself but was created by God for our good, and we should not do things in this world that will ruin our lives. Then people will have more goodness than they can imagine and as much as they can possibly have.

Faith

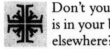 Don't you know that the source of life is in your body? Why do you look for it elsewhere? When you do this, you are like a man who burns a lamp in daylight.

False religion tells us to deny this life for life eternal. Eternal life already exists; it is a part of this present life. — INDIAN PROVERB

When we find religion, we stop looking for individual purposes and can walk together along the path of life by understanding there is one common law, one origin, and one purpose.

Religion existed before Christianity. It began when people had their first religious aspirations and has existed ever since. Just as there is one big world ocean, there is only one true religion; but we nevertheless think true believers are only the ones who belong to our church.

— THEODORE PARKER

Soul

If a child does not know he has a heart, this does not mean he doesn't have one. The same is true of the spiritual. If a person does not feel his spirit inside him, it does not mean he is without one.

A person does not truly know himself. What he thinks of as himself is not his true self, for a person does not live by the body but by his spirit.

Every being moves jointly with all other beings, yet at the same time, his conscience is motionless. Our life is found in this contradiction.

If there is to be motion in life, then this motion occurs in relation to something that does not move. This motionless thing is the eternal spirit inside us that observes the life around it.

One Soul in All

If there is something similar about all men, it is the spirit. If this is so, we should respect this spirit inside all of us.

An Indian wise man once said, "The spirit of life is in you, and in me, and in every other human being. You should not be angry with me when I approach to talk. Also, you should not be proud, no matter how high the position you occupy."

Some people are separated from others by riches, glory, or rank and can never be serene or joyful. Yet as soon as they recognize their inner spirit, to them all people will become as family and they will grasp that there is something inside more precious than anything else in the world.

Why do we have such a feeling of awe when a person dies? We are able to see that which is changing its form into a different state, and we can glimpse this in ourselves when we see it happening in another.

God

One day, a fish heard people saying that fish can live only in the water. At this, many different fish started asking each other, "Does anyone know what water is?" They decided to ask the oldest and the wisest fish, who answered, "Water is by what we live, and in what we live. You do not know water, because you live in it." In the same way, some people do not know God, but we all live by God and in God, and God lives in us.

Why does the spiritual "me" not want to stay in my body forever? It was put in my body not by my will but by the superior will that I call God.

People who live bad lives say, "There is no God." They are right. God is the highest perfection for those who can see him and desire to draw closer to Him. For those who turn their back on Him and go away from Him, there is no God.

Unification in Spirit

Until a man is truly alive, he will always want something — respect, wealth, entertainment, or thousands of other things. The reality is that he wants only one thing — to be connected to and not separated from other people. We all are united by that which is the same in all people: the divine spirit.

Unification is a force. We all know this. Then why is it so weak, when it can be stronger than anything else?

Many, especially the young, like to say that they are all alone and nobody loves them. As soon as they can understand our spiritual unity with others, they will have a feeling of constant joy.

"God is love. Whoever lives in love lives in God, and God in him. No one has ever seen God; but if we love one another, God lives in us and His love is made complete in us. . . . Dear friends, let us love one another, for love comes from God." — 1 John 4:16, 12, 7

Universal Love

If you are trying to determine whether an action is good or bad, you have only to ask yourself if it will increase the love between people. If the answer is yes and love grows, it is good.

Love your enemies, and you won't have any.

To have perfect love, we should strive for perfection, that is, to love God. Since God lives in everyone's spirit, we should love all people.

Love destroys death, brings sense to life, and turns unhappiness into happiness.

"Love God with all your heart, with all your emotion." True life is found only in love. Only those who love are truly alive.

A new love is like a new shoot on a tree. Frail and tender when it appears, it will grow if lit by sunshine, love, and intellect.

Sin

 You cannot force yourself to love another person. This does not mean there is no love inside you but that there is an obstacle to love.

Sinning is our job. Making up excuses and explaining away our sins is the devil's job.

Temptation is not just a temporary event, as in, you live your life and then suddenly encounter a temptation. No, temptation is a constant companion in your moral inner life.

The further you go along the path of a good life, the more temptations you will encounter and need to confront. Temptations are like entering a swamp; you must extract yourself quickly.

To eliminate your biggest sins, first start with the small temptations. If you cling to your fame, glory, or importance, you will never be able to rid yourself of other bad things.

Temptation

If you want to live a free and happy life, do not seek superfluities, like wealth or luxury, but try to make due with only the necessary.

When we teach our children to become accustomed to excessive food, luxury, or laziness, we are preparing them for a future of physical suffering.

Your thirst for emotions and desires binds you. If you can rid yourself of this thirst, then your suffering will fall away from you as raindrops fall from the lotus flower.   — BUDDHIST WISDOM

The more you satisfy your body's demands, the weaker your spiritual force becomes. The wise and the saintly always live celibate, ascetic lives.

Work and Idleness

It is a shame when a person is advised to work as hard as an ant. And it is twice the shame when he does not follow this advice. — THE TALMUD

Manual labor is the duty and means of happiness for all. Intellectual and imaginative work is the exception, but only for those who have the special gifts required.

Most of the activity of the idle is considered by them to be hard work, but in reality it is just entertainment.

People jump from one pleasure to another when they feel their lives are empty. But they do not yet feel the emptiness of the entertainment currently attracting them. — BLAISE PASCAL

Greed and Wealth

Wealth, not poverty, is the true burden.

Enormous wealth is a sin, because for every rich person there are hundreds in poverty.

It is obvious that the more you give to others and the less you ask for yourself, the better off you are. Even so, people find many different excuses not to follow this rule.

Charitable institutions can be useless or even harmful. They can sometimes be useful, but they can never be moral. The very existence of these institutions shows us the existence of human suffering.

The selfishness of rich people is not as cruel as their lack of compassion.

— JEAN-JACQUES ROUSSEAU

Desire and Passion

A person can struggle with his lustful physical state but still desire to live a loving life. The same can be seen in his sexual life. A physically driven person will produce children but may also wish that he was, or had been, celibate. Our physical and spiritual sides are in conflict with each other.

An honest marriage is good, but celibacy is better.

The struggle with sexual sin is a difficult one. We can be completely free of it only in early childhood or our old age.

Blessed is the childhood that among the cruel lives on this earth gives us a little bit of heaven.

If the Christian ideal could be fulfilled, we would have no more executions, wars, or poverty. People would rapidly multiply, for as true Christians, their marriages would produce children. The world could have become overpopulated if it had not been for the Christian teaching of celibacy.

193

Anger and Hatred

 A wise man is not one who makes nice speeches but one who is patient, free of hatred, and free from fear. Only one who follows this path is a wise man.

— BUDDHIST PROVERB

To cast aside your hostility toward others, remind yourself that if someone does a bad thing and is not ashamed of it, he is blind and he cannot tell good from evil. In this way, most people are innocent.

People like to point out each other's flaws, and by doing so they show their own weakness. The wiser and kinder a person is, the more good he sees in others.

Every time a person abuses or harms you and you feel hostile toward this person, remind yourself that we all have the same spirit of God, no matter who you dislike.

If you cannot forgive your brother, you do not love him. True love has no limits.

Thoughts

 A sin does not stop being a sin if many people sin this way and are proud of it.

Those who do not think independently are under another's influence. To always have to live out the thoughts of others is the worst slavery imaginable, worse than the slavery of the body.

Do what you think is good, and don't rely on the standards of others.

Those who are ashamed of what they should not be ashamed of, step onto the path headed for destruction.   — BUDDHIST PROVERB

Our inner conscience holds more meaning than the outside world's judgments, because we will live with our consciences forever, for all eternity.

Judgment and Punishment

Our leaders want to fight evil with evil — with punishments, prisons, executions, and so on. However, doing so only makes the punishers and the punished more and more cruel.

Imagine thinking that a group of people is bad and that you can improve them by force. They may in turn think the same about you. Why improve them and not yourself?

It may appear that violence brings justice, but it only seems that way. In reality, the only thing that leads to justice is living a free life.

Why is most religion perverted, and why is morality in decline? There is only one reason: it is because people believe in living a life based on violence.

The prejudice of violence passes from one generation to the next and continues its harm. People brought up with violence grow used to the idea that their adult lives should be filled with it.

Violence and War

Each act of violence not only fails to calm us down but brings increasingly more violence into our lives. Therefore, it is clear that we cannot change or improve our lives through violence. We lash out for revenge, not self-improvement.

Not only Christ but all the wise men in the world — Buddhist, Brahman, Taoist, and the ancient Greeks — taught that intelligent people should respond with good to evil.

It is clear that violence and murder make people indignant, and yet they repay violence and murder with more violence and murder. Obviously, there is an explanation for this response, but there is no way we can justify it.

The teaching of peace is a natural consequence of the teaching of love.

Pride

People think that loving a family member or your neighbor is a virtue. It is, and there is nothing wrong with it. However, if you harm those far from you for the sake of those near to you, this is not right. For example, if you steal from others to feed your family or go to war and kill other people, then this virtue has become a vice.

Living for your spirit is different than living for the material world. First of all, if you live for your soul, you cannot feel content with yourself, no matter how much good you do.

It is good to respect yourself for the sake of the divine spirit living within you, but you should not feel pride over such matters as intelligence, education, origin, riches, or even your good deeds.

Four major temptations torture people: pride, lust, anger or divisiveness, and the desire for fame. We can resist them all by improving ourselves.

Violence and War

 Many of the bad things people do, they do for themselves. Much worse things people do for their families. However, the most terrible deeds are done for their government and country — deception, war, spying, and killing others.

Murder is always murder, no matter why you have to kill. People who promote murder are evil even if they are judges or generals. They also are criminals. We should pity them and reeducate them.

For a wise man, his being is his homeland. He feels good wherever he goes, because his happiness is found within himself, in his spirit.

We can remove the filth from our body with soap. The same thing can be done in our communities: they too should be cleansed.

Faith

If a person never really thinks about his faith, he will believe that the only true religion is the one he was brought up in. But what if you were born a Muslim, a Buddhist, or a Hindu? Religion does not become true just because you say yours is the only true one.

The most harmful lies are the sophisticated ones, and these are most often lies about religion.

True religion is nothing more than the moral rules and laws that we understand with our intellect and our conscience.

Your faith is established from the inside, not the outside.

Prayer as a formal religious ritual is a mistake. Our true spiritual prayer is the desire of our heart to draw closer to God and to please Him.

— IMMANUEL KANT

False Science

 A Persian wise man once said, "When I was young, I wanted to know about science. I then learned almost everything a person could know. When I grew old and looked at everything I had learned, I knew my life had passed and I knew nothing."

False science and religion use ultrarefined and sophisticated language, so that people who do not know the truth will believe they are very serious and important.

A mysterious façade is not a quality of wisdom.　— LUCY MALLORY

The wiser a person is, the simpler the language he will use to express his thoughts.

Two qualities of a true scientist are: first, when a scholar works for his inner satisfaction, not profit; second, when it is obvious to the observer that there is good in his science.

Effort

If you do only what you want, you will not do it for long without becoming bored. If you want to do a really good thing, you have to make an effort to finish it.

You say that you might as well not make an effort, because no matter how many good things you do, you can never achieve perfection. Your purpose is not to be perfect, but to eliminate as many temptations and prejudices as possible. You can achieve this only with effort.

You can save yourself only by making an effort, by waking up from your previous life as from a bad dream.

Your moral effort and joy in life are analagous to physical labor and the subsequent joy found in rest. Without labor, there is no joy in repose. Without a moral effort, there is no joy to understanding this life.

Self-Sacrifice

 If a person lives for his spirit, then self-denial will be easy for him.

If a person is self-centered and looks out only for himself, he cannot be truly happy. If you truly want to live for yourself, live for others.

People find their purpose in seeking a higher position, a larger salary, or greater wealth or fame and then spend their whole life in pursuit of it. Yet goodness in life comes from communicating with others, from the most casual conversation to the discussion of difficult matters, when you feel at one with them. When you do this, you can see how your life will become free and joyful.

There are three states in which your spirit cannot be touched by sin, temptation, or prejudice. They are denying yourself in your body, remaining humble when tempted, and maintaining truth over prejudice.

Humility and Modesty

To be truly humble is difficult, for one resists the thought of being humbled. However, no matter how difficult, it is possible. Try to remove this obstacle to humility.

The person making an effort to become humble resembles a man who goes from the basement into bright daylight. The higher he climbs, the more light he sees.

The more you think about your inner self, the less important you are to yourself and the more humble you become. Therefore, be meek and you will become wise.

Self-confidence is a quality of animals, and humility a quality of man.

Truth

You cannot tell a lie without adding another to it. Remember this, and be afraid of even the smallest, most innocent of lies. Unimportant things can lead to important consequences.

Nothing can distract people from truth more than just mechanically repeating what other people do and say.

The more you question your actions with your intellect, the freer your life becomes.

Why is the perversion of the truth used only for achieving selfish ends?

If the truth does not tell us what we should do, it will always tell us what we should *not* do in order to live a good life.

Desire and Passion

 Do not do the things that you should not do, and you will do those that you should.

If you give in to your passionate desires and start seeking pleasure, your passions will grow stronger and stronger, and you will wrap yourself in chains in the long run.

Look at how people live in this world. Look at Chicago, Paris, and London, and all the cities, planes, trains, cars, armies with their weapons, fortresses, temples, museums, and high-rise buildings. Then ask yourself the question, "What should we do so that all people live a better life?" You will have the answer: First of all, we shouldn't do whatever is bad or unnecessary, which is mostly what we are doing now.

Who are the rich? Those who are happy with what they have. Who are the strong? Those who can control their emotions. — THE TALMUD

Words

 The words you do not speak out loud are pure gold.

You bear God's spirit. You can express a part of the divine with words. Why then are you not careful of what you say?

In an argument, you are not arguing for truth but for yourself. — THOMAS CARLYLE

Words are the expressions of thoughts, and thoughts the expressions of divine power. Therefore, let your words correspond to what they express. Be careful with them. They cannot be emotionless, nor should they convey evil.

Time may pass, but a word spoken remains.

Thoughts

If a person can think, he can understand why he is alive. The opposite is also true. If a person cannot think, he cannot understand why he is alive. If he cannot understand this, he cannot understand what is good and what is bad. Therefore, it is important to think properly.

I had a thought and then forgot it. It's all right, it's only just a thought. If it were a million rubles, I would make a huge effort to find it, but it's just a thought. Yet a thought can be the seed of a huge tree of the future. A good thought can make a good impact on a person, or on millions of people.

One of our greatest faculties is intellect. Just like the other faculties, though, if we do not exercise it, we can lose it. Those who do not exercise their intellect do not feel it in itself.

Beware of words, beware of thoughts, beware bad actions. If you do this, you will walk the path of a wise man.

Living in the Present

 When a person wants to, he can have a good life now, without thinking about what will happen when his life is over. A person can be happy when he fulfills the law of God.

Do not postpone a good deed, if you can do it now. Death will not ask you what you have done and what you have left to do. Therefore, the most important thing for a person is what you are doing right now.

If we could only grasp that we cannot return to the past and fix the evil we have done, then we would understand that we should do more good things, and fewer bad.

The consequences of your actions will be judged by others. You should act from your heart, and do pure and truthful things.

You already possess everything you want to have. At any moment in your life, you can do what you think necessary.

There Is No Evil

There is a story from the Old Testament that a man was punished for his sins by losing the ability to die. You can truly see that if a person is punished so he won't suffer or feel anymore, this punishment is as bad as the first one.

Bodily changes, illness, loss, or death are not in your power to control. What happens to your inner life, your spirit, *is* within your power. If I follow the will of God, I feel good inside, no matter what happens on the outside.

Fire can both destroy and provide warmth. Illness is the same. I can feel joyful when I am sick. During an illness, the burden of everyday concerns disappears, and when I am cured, I once again feel this pressure.

Remember that the reason for your suffering is within you.

Death

 Memento mori, "Remember that you must die," is a great expression. If we remembered that we will all die, our lives would hold a different meaning. The person who thinks he will die in half an hour will not do anything stupid.

Only thoughts will set you free, and after I've thought it over, I can say that death is the greatest one I know.

The actions of a dying person have great impact on other people. Therefore, it is important to live well but even more important to die well.

A good honest death can redeem a bad life.

After Death

 Soul does not live in a body as in a house. It is more like a traveler who stayed in a small tavern along the road.

— INDIAN KURAL

We often try to imagine death as a passage to the other side. But this is as impossible as imagining God.

All you can believe is that everything that comes from God, including death, is good.

If you look at a human life from birth to death, you can compare it to a single day, when you woke up in the morning and went to bed at nightfall.

When a voice is telling us that we are eternal, it is the voice of God living in us.

Happiness

You can give a man everything he wants — wealth, fame, health — but he will nevertheless be unhappy if he does not live his life according to God's will. The opposite is also true. You can take a man's wealth, fame, and health from him, and he will still be happy if he lives his life according to God's will.

To be happy, to live eternal life, to live in God's spirit, to be saved — all this is the same thing. This is the task for your life.

A wise man does not seek to change his position in life, because he knows it is possible to fulfill God's will in any circumstances.

The meaning of a life cannot be determined by its suffering, or its longevity or short span. It comes in striving for spiritual perfection, which is always possible.

Faith

 The stronger your faith, the more solid your life will be.

"Who am I? What am I? What can I expect from life?" These are the three major questions we need to ask. The most important is the question, "What am I?" which is closely joined to the question, "What should I do?" If you know what you are, you will know what to do, and what to expect. If you know your work is to love others, then you should focus only on loving.

The commandment of Christ, "Love God and your neighbor," is very clear and simple. Everyone can understand it in his heart. If there were no false religious teachings, people would have followed this law and the kingdom of God would have come to earth. Therefore, do not believe any teaching that does not allow us to love God and our neighbor.

To know true faith, do not abandon your intellect as false teachers tell you, but use your intellect to test your faith. Make every effort to do this.

Soul

 To be a fully complete human being, you have to realize that God lives in you.

If you can agree that the eternal world really exists, you can accept that other eternal things also exist, such as your own spiritual beginning, through which you understand this world.

Your conscience gives you the ability to understand your spiritual origin. This is the best indicator of what should you do.

What a joy — discovering the divine spirit within you! How can we not rejoice in this fact?

I hear footsteps at my door. I hear the words, "It's me." I ask, "Who is it?" The answer is again, "It's me." It is the farmer's son who lives next door. He is surprised. He is talking about his inner spiritual "me," and I am talking to a small window through which one can see the world.

One Soul in All

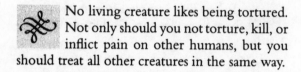 No living creature likes being tortured. Not only should you not torture, kill, or inflict pain on other humans, but you should treat all other creatures in the same way.

The wiser and kinder a person is, the more he can see himself in others. Only stupid and cruel people think others are "alien" to them.

The teachers of mankind possessed wisdom and saintlike abilities, which anyone can possess, for a spiritual force resides in each of us.

We can feel true compassion only when we put ourselves in the place of a person who is suffering.

God

 I am not afraid to live my life when I am walking alongside God. Without Him, I am afraid.

God is like the x in a mathematical equation. We cannot compute the equation without the x. Life gives you the solution to this equation.

A mathematician was once asked what he thought of God. He replied, "I never needed this hypothesis." If the same question were put to me, I would answer, "Without this hypothesis, I cannot think logically about anything."

If one day you have the thought that all you have believed about God is not true and does not exist, do not be ashamed of this. Everyone can have such thoughts. Thinking there is something wrong in your belief in God will help you to better understand or think about the things that you call "God."

Unification in Spirit

 The ancient wise man Seneca once said that all the people around us are the members of one human body. Like hands, legs, stomach, and bones, together we make up the parts of the same body. We are all born in the same way and have similar features. We are like the stones that make up an arch. We can be destroyed if we do not support each other.

You want to do what is good, yet you move hastily, because you do not know you are moving in the wrong direction or that right beside you is a huge river of love flowing in one eternal direction. Stop your irrational movements, and jump into the river of love. It will carry you, and you will feel calm and free.

People are unhappy when everyone lives for themselves. If they lived according to the law we were taught by the wise men, they could all be happy. This law? "Treat others as you want to be treated."

Universal Love

 True love occurs only when you love everyone, not just those you like.

Love gives, wanting nothing in return.

You should be like a glass bowl, inside of which is a lamp of God. If the glass is clean and clear, the lamp will shine brightly, and you will feel unlimited joy.

There is a natural kindness that you are brought up with. Based on what you ate for dinner, or on your success, this type of kindness can soon disappear. Another kind of kindness is based on your spiritual life. This type of kindness is constantly growing, and will endow you with goodness more and more.

True love, seen not in words but in deeds, can appear stupid. In the end, however, it is only this love that gives you wisdom.

Sin

 Sin, temptation, and prejudice are the fertilizers for the seeds of love that help love to sprout and grow.

Sin, temptation, and prejudice need to exist in this world; otherwise our lives would not develop. Our purpose in life is to set ourselves free from them.

The origin of your bodily sins is found in your body. The cause of your passions is found in obedience to other people. The reason for your prejudices is found in lies.

People are punished not for their sins, but by their sins, which is the most difficult punishment.

Sin

 The sins of pleasing your body are natural in children. But in adults, especially the elderly, these sins are disgusting: wanting exquisite foods, wearing excessive makeup or costly clothes, desiring a huge house to live in or great entertainments to relax with.

The more needs you satisfy, the more enslaved you become, because the more you need, the less freedom you have.

Complete freedom is found in desiring nothing. The next step is to need a little.
— JOHN CHRISTENDOM

No one ever drank alcohol in order to do good things — to work, ponder life, care for the sick, or pray to God. Most bad things are done under the influence of alcohol.

Desire and Passion

When should people get married? If a man and a woman both think it would be difficult for them to live without each other — then should they get married.

Good marriages produce good children.

It is not true that celibacy goes against human nature. Celibacy is possible when your life is dedicated to God. This can occur even in marriage, if both partners have dedicated their lives to God.

When a person falls into a sexual affair once, he will sooner or later fall into others, and over time can even lose the ability to truly love. He will feel hatred, disgust, and despair and enter a living hell.

Work and Idleness

 Do not ask others to do the things you can do yourself.

Everyone should clean their own thresholds and the entrance to their houses. If everyone cleaned their front yards, then the whole street would look clean and neat.

One of the body's greatest joys is to rest after physical labor. All the entertainment in the world cannot compare to this.

It is a terrible mistake to think that the human spirit can live a highly elevated spiritual life, while your body remains in idleness and luxury. Your body is the first student of your soul.

— HENRY DAVID THOREAU

Greed and Wealth

 The joys that wealth brings are deceitful and changing.

Someone with only a little is not poor. The poor one is the one who wants more than he already has. — SENECA

Support for the poor with material things or money is good only when it's a sacrifice. Only then will the one who gave receive a spiritual gift and a blessing. However, when you merely discard your abundance, it isn't heartfelt and can irritate those who receive it.

There is something wrong with the order of this world when the rich live off the labors of the poor. They are fed by them, live in the houses they build, and are served by them — and if that isn't enough, they establish charities for them and think themselves their benefactors.

Anger and Hatred

 Anger can be harmful mostly to the person who is angry, because anger is not worth whatever you are angry about.

There are people who will harm others for no reason. An evil person seems to me to be insane.

If you are angry with someone, you try to justify your feelings with the bad qualities of the person you are angry at. Instead try the opposite — seek the good things in that person. Then you will feel less anger and distress and more pleasure and satisfaction.

Sometimes you cannot help being angry at a person. However, always try not to express your bad mood either in your words or your actions.

Pride

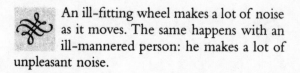 An ill-fitting wheel makes a lot of noise as it moves. The same happens with an ill-mannered person: he makes a lot of unpleasant noise.

It is difficult to love everyone all the time, but this does not mean you shouldn't make an effort. Every good thing is difficult.

Self-love is the beginning of pride; pride is the culmination of loving only yourself.

Try to direct all your good qualities toward helping others. If you are strong, support the weak. If you are wise, help those who are not. If you are well educated, help those who have no education. If you are rich, help the poor. However, those who are proud think differently. They think that if they have something others do not, they should hold themselves above others and not share it.

Effort

When I do not understand myself, then I live the life of an animal. When I understand my life and do what I have decided, then I live a human life. When I understand the life of others and love them, then I live a godly life.

Goodness without life is impossible. How can I find goodness? Only in this life. For example, I was looking for fresh mushrooms, which could be found only in the forest. If I wanted to collect mushrooms, why would I leave the forest?

A wise word spoken to a drunken pauper can have more far-reaching consequences than sophisticated works of art: we do not know the true consequences of our actions.

I have a very important thing to do — to die properly. This is also very important for everyone. To die properly, you must live a good life. You will not remember this at the age of twenty-five, but at eighty-one you will understand it quite well.

Judgment and Punishment

People do many bad things to each other because they are weak and sinful. One such thing is to punish others. Only God should punish people.

People come up with different explanations for why they believe in punishment. In most cases, they simply want to repay evil to those who have harmed them.

"You have heard the saying, 'An eye for an eye, a tooth for a tooth.' But I tell you, do not resist evil." These words show how Jesus not only rejected violence but also disagreed with its being the central law of society. He advocated love for all people without exception, and spoke of a new world based on this principle of unconditional love.

Nothing can give people more joy than being forgiven for the evil they have done. It is joyful for both those who forgive and those who receive the forgiveness offered.

Violence and War

 If we need to force people to obey justice by using violence, it is not true justice. — BLAISE PASCAL

In our day it is difficult to find someone who would kill a defenseless person, yet what else happens in capital punishment?

When people beat their children, they try to make them behave properly by using violence and force. When someone is sentenced to death, we are trying to improve our world through capital punishment. When one nation declares war on another, it is trying to improve its position. How strange that violence always leads to disappointment in the long run.

Real life happens not in our grand deeds, or when we move, clash, or go to war but in the small, hardly noticeable changes that take place in our souls.

Humility and Modesty

When a person is truly clever, he does not know it, for it just seems natural to understand things. When a person is truly kind, he does not notice his kindness, because he knows he could always be kinder. Therefore, a clever and kind person is always humble.

Live like you have nothing to hide and nothing to boast about in a crowd.

Ask anyone, pilgrims and travelers from near and far, if there is anything more important than truth, love, and humility. — BUDDHIST WISDOM

Only humility stops everything that builds obstacles in the way of peace for all.

Faith

 Many false laws are considered to be the laws of God. There is only one true law of God.

People ask for fresh bread, fresh butter, and fresh eggs — because they know that fresh food is healthier. When we talk about religion, the older the spiritual food, the more precious it is.
— LUCY MALLORY

Religion comes from God, but religious explanations and commentaries come from people.

The institution of church is always dictatorial, no matter what outer forms it takes. It does not convince you, but gives you directions on how to behave. — IMMANUEL KANT

False Science

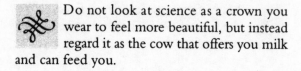 Do not look at science as a crown you wear to feel more beautiful, but instead regard it as the cow that offers you milk and can feed you.

Science is found to be good only when it helps you become a better person.

Science should feed your intellect. Either it can be good for you, as good food is for your stomach, or it can be bad for you, when it is not fresh or clean or you overindulge in it.

A scholar is a person who may have spent a long period of time learning, but this does not mean he has learned anything or that he is clever enough to do so.   — GEORGE C. LICHTENBERG

Effort

To do something properly, you must know how to do it. This concerns any activity. To live a good life, you must learn how to live a good life. To do this, you must make an effort.

Hope that we will attain the kingdom of God isn't enough. We know it will come, for it comes to us every day, every day that we make a good effort.

We often want to do great, important things. Yet we should not try to achieve anything great, only that which God's spirit, dwelling in us, tells us to do.

Thinking that you can change some small aspect of your life and it will suddenly become better is thinking as some children do: that by sitting on a carpet and tugging on its ends, you can fly.

One Soul in All

"Love your neighbor as yourself" does not mean that you have to make a heroic effort to love your neighbor. You cannot force yourself to love. It seems that when you stop loving yourself more than others, then you will naturally love others as much as yourself.

Military personnel know that it is possible to die for others, and some do so with ease. Then, why is a person who thinks he can serve God not ready to die for others?

If you truly love God, you would not ask Him to love you in return. It is simply enough to love God.

A farmer's cow feeds you and your children with milk, and his sheep keep you warm with their wool for many years. What is their reward? Cut their throats, and eat them.

Humility and Modesty

The prouder you think you are, the weaker you become. The more humble you are, the stronger you are, and the firmer you stand.

It is bad when you think of yourself as good, because you will not do the most necessary thing, which is to improve yourself.

Every day, make an effort.

True love is possible only when you are humble.

You can see your faults only through the eyes of others.

Truth

 The consequences of telling a lie far exceed in harm and unpleasantness whatever temporary gain we may achieve.

Do not give in to your passions or to false opinion. Both lead to a life filled with lies.

The majority of our actions are guided by the force of other people's opinions and teachings.

You think, "My life is always running somewhere, as if it is running away from me. Where can I find the truth?" You have an inner voice you should listen to. It is the voice of the truth that lives inside you.

— ALEXANDER GERTZEN

The most important thing every person can do is to live a good life. This is achieved not only by doing good but more importantly by not doing bad things. Yes, the most important is not to do bad things.

Actions

Many things happening in the world around us are outside of our control. If God wants something to happen in a different way than we have planned, it means He wanted it to happen that way. We should try not to go against the will of God.

We should not just try to be good but actually embody goodness in our actions.

If you truly want to be free, curb your desires.

What is the best thing to do when you are in a hurry? The answer: Nothing.

You may not know exactly what to do in a specific moment, but you do know exactly what you should not do. By avoiding what you should not do, you will inevitably start doing the things you should do in order to lead a good life.

Words

 Do not listen to those who speak ill of one another and good of you.

The best way to attract the love of others is to ignore their flaws and talk only about their good qualities.

If you want to judge me, you have to do so by putting yourself in my position. For kind people, it is difficult to imagine that others can be evil. Evil people, in the same way, find it difficult to imagine that others can be good.

The truth is lost during an argument.

The wiser person is the one who is the first to stop an argument.

Thoughts

It would be good if wisdom could be poured from a very wise person into one who has little wisdom, just as water can be poured from one vessel to another. However, in order to accept the wisdom of others, you need to make the effort to think.

All things that are necessary for people, such as intelligence and faith, are not given to them all at once but are achieved over time and by constant work.

To live a good and kind life, you need to make yourself think good thoughts.

A person can achieve spiritual perfection only with intellectual effort.

There is only one kind of treasure that does not get smaller when you give it to others. You can give away as much as you want, and it only grows bigger. It is the treasure of wisdom.

Living in the Present

 Nothing is important except for what you are doing in this particular moment, because only this moment truly belongs to you.

You only truly live in the present. You have the ability to remember the past, and to imagine the future, but these abilities are given to us only so we can do a good job in the present.

The closer you want to become to God, the more you should concentrate on the present. The opposite is also true.

"Tomorrow will take care of itself," said Jesus. This is a great truth. The beauty of life is that you don't know what is good for the future. Only one thing is good and necessary — to love others, now, in the present.

There Is No Evil

 It is only in suffering that we truly start living through our soul.

We should reveal to a sick person that his sickness will soon lead to death. If we fail to do this, we take away the good given to him by his sickness, for he will not know to prepare for death.

Those who are blind, crippled, deaf, or dumb may think they are less fortunate and happy than others. Our happiness lies not in our body but in our spirit. The weakest person can have more spiritual inner strength than the person with the strongest physical body.

In the same way the night sky reveals the stars, our suffering reveals to us the meaning of life.

Death

To live a good life and do good, remind yourself often that sooner or later you will die. Imagine you will die tomorrow, and you will find that you stop lying, feeling jealous, scolding or judging people, or stealing from them.

Love destroys not only the fear of death but even the thought of death.

If you perform acts of love, you will not die.

I love my garden. I love to read a good book. I love to hug little children. When I am dead, I will lose all this. I do not want to die, and I am afraid of death. But then, suddenly, I understood that all of my desires must be replaced by one — to fulfill the will of God.

After Death

 You can look at life as a dream, and death as an awakening.

He who understands that he will not be destroyed after death is eternal. — LAO-TZU

Atheism indicates that a person has some intellect but only to a certain limited extent. Both the truly wise and the completely stupid are not atheists.

Who gave me my life in this place and time? Life reminds me of a very brief day I spent visiting someone. — BLAISE PASCAL

They say there will be a day of judgment on the last day, and God will be angry. However, God is truly kind, and nothing can come from God except goodness and kindness. So be not afraid: in both your present life, and your afterlife, nothing may happen except kindness and goodness. — PERSIAN PROVERB

Happiness

Wise men are always happy.

There are very few things that are truly good that are good for all of us. Therefore, we should desire these things.

We should live in our spiritual life and devote all our efforts to it. This is similar to having the wings of a bird. We can and should live in our physical life, but as soon as an obstacle appears, we should spread our wings and start to fly.

We are all like wild horses put in harness for the first time. In the beginning, we try to run away, break the harness, and live for ourselves. But over time we become tired, forget about our own will, submit to the superior will, and pull our load. We then feel calm and satisfied.

People should remember that the world did not come into existence by itself but was created by God for our good, and we should not do things in this world that ruin our lives. Then people will have more goodness than they can imagine and as much as they can possibly have.

Faith

"Love each other, as I have loved you. By this, all others will know that you are my students if you love each other," said Jesus. He did not say, "if you believe" in this or that, but "if you love." People can believe different things, and still have the same love.

True worship of God is when you expect no reward in return. — AGNI PURANA

Faith is a necessary quality of your inner self. Besides what we do know, we find ourselves relating to things we do not know but for the fact they exist. This relationship to the unknown origin is faith.

Very often you see people who will sacrifice everything, for example in war or by committing suicide; yet you will seldom find people willing to give their life for truth. The reason for this is that it is easy to forfeit your life based on the convictions of the crowd, but difficult to do so for truth alone.

Soul

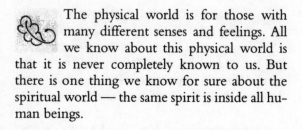 The physical world is for those with many different senses and feelings. All we know about this physical world is that it is never completely known to us. But there is one thing we know for sure about the spiritual world — the same spirit is inside all human beings.

You will be able to find the way out of any difficult situation, if you know that God lives in you.

"Me," according to my senses and my body, is a link between my ancestors and descendants, just a temporary piece of flesh. What really exists is my inner self, my inner spirit. This is the real "me."

A drop, when it gets to the ocean, becomes a part of the ocean. Your soul, when it unites with God, becomes a part of God.

— ANGELUS SILESIUS

One Soul in All

There is a connection between me and all people, living and dead. I feel I need those people, and they need me. Together, I live with them, and they live with me. We should think the same about animals, even insects. Remember that the same spirit is living in us all. We should teach ourselves compassion even for the insects. The more we feel pity and love, the happier and better our lives will be.

A bee is just a bee, a fly is just a fly, but they are alive, and each has a little bit of what I have. The same can be said of a tree, and a stone. As for a tree, I can feel it a little bit; as for a stone, I can only imagine that it is there.

The great joys you feel when you show kindness to animals far outweigh the small pleasures you get from eating meat and hunting.

God

Moses said to God, "Where can I find you, my Lord?" And God said, "If you are looking for me, you have already found me." — FROM THE ARABIC

A wise person was once asked, "How do you know that God exists?" He answered, "Do you need a candle to see the sunrise?"

God is without limits, and we can draw closer to Him in unlimited ways.

When you have doubts about God, look for a deeper understanding. You will then understand Him even better, and instead of being filled with doubt, your faith will become stronger.

The part of me that has no material body I call spirit. The part of the world that has no material representation I call God.

Unification in Spirit

The same thing can be good for one person and bad for another. A city devoured by an earthquake or covered by lava from volcano, or crops destroyed by storms — we cannot say if it was a good or bad occurrence, because we do not know what else could have happened.

A clever and thoughtful person can see the power of God even in the smallest and least significant things happening around him.

It only seems humanity is busy with trade, laws, society, science, and the arts. In fact, humanity truly does only one thing — it tries to understand the moral laws by which it lives, that bind people together.

Universal Love

The best person among us all is the person who loves and treats everyone with goodness, without thinking about who is good or bad. — MUHAMMAD

Authentic teachers tell us that love is the essence of life. It lives in our souls. People who live through love live a good life.

To live a godly life, all you must do is love.

Love is nothing other than understanding that others are also "me."

When a person is alone — in the desert, in prison, or anywhere he is truly alone — he can follow the law by loving God and all He is revealed to be. A person can do this even in his memories, dreams, or thoughts.

Sin

Being in a bad mood is harmful for others but can be useful to you when you are working in solitude on your inner perfection.

The person who sins for the first time feels guilty. The person who repeats the same sin many times becomes used to it and regards it as something he is allowed to do.

A lost person finds joy in his sins. A wise person finds joy in being set free from them.

If you confess and turn away from your sins, this means you understand your sins and are ready to fight them. It is good to do this while you have enough energy. You should put more oil in the lamp while it is burning.

People sometimes use their intellect to justify the bad things they've done. To use your intellect this way is called temptation.

Desire and Passion

If people could attain perfection, they would become celibate, and the human race would die out. People would be like angels that do not marry, as it says in the New Testament. However, we are not perfect, and we keep on producing children.

You become connected to the earthly things, as a suckling calf is connected to its mother, when you feel sexual attraction for another. Those with such sexual desires are like a rabbit caught in a trap. The rabbit has ropes all around it, but still it makes convulsive jumps, getting caught tighter in the ropes. — BUDDHIST PROVERB

If you father a child, then it is your child. The woman who gave birth to this child is the child's mother, and together you make a family.

When people concentrate sexual energy on love affairs, they end up wasting their energy for harmful purposes.

Work and Idleness

Where there is one lazy person, there is another person who works for him. Where there is one person who has more than enough, there is another who hungers, lacking the most basic necessities.

All smoking and alcoholic beverages that stupefy us were created by idle people for the main purpose of ridding themselves of boredom.

When you do not work, you become bored. When you are bored, you sin.

If your life has a job that is relieved by rest and pleasure, with a repetitive cycle of work and pleasure, your life is joyful. But this is not true of every job, or every pleasure.

Greed and Wealth

A Chinese wise man once said, "When a poor man is jealous of a rich man, it is not very good, but it can be explained. But if a rich person tries to raise himself above others and does not want to share his riches with the poor, this is not good, and cannot be excused."

Robbing the rich on a highway does not happen as often as robbing the poor these days, because it is dangerous to rob the rich but easy to rob the poor without any risk. — John Ruskin

Wealth is the reward for hard work. Usually one person performs the work, and another reaps the reward. This is called by educated people the division of labor.

There is something more egregious than a lack of justice. This is the hypocrisy of those who just pretend to be good.

Anger and Hatred

When two people fight, both are to blame, for while they are fighting, they do not love each other and are angry with each other.

As soon as you are angry with another person, ask yourself, "Why is he doing this to me?" When you understand this, you cannot stay angry with that person, any more than you could be angry with a falling stone.

You can see a person's progress toward goodness when he does not strike back when he is hit, or when he does not respond with a bad word when one is spoken to him.

All anger comes from weakness.
— JEAN-JACQUES ROUSSEAU

Pride

 Look for a good person among those who are judged by the world.

When a person loves only a select few, he loves with a human love. For a truly divine love, all people should be loved equally.

Thinking yourself better than others is stupid and not morally good. Thinking your family is better than others is even more stupid. Thinking your nation is better than the rest is the worst idea you can think up. However, some don't think of this as bad, and consider pride a great virtue.

A wise man said that the most important thing is to understand your own self. A proud person is then far from wisdom. He cannot understand himself, because he does not want to know what kind of person he really is.

Vanity and Fame

 We would be much stronger if we did not pay attention to fame.

If you want to be happy, try only to please God, not people. Each person will want different things, as they are all different. Moreover, some will want something today, while others will want something tomorrow. Yet God wants only one thing, and you know in your heart what that is.

Even if you have made some great achievement, you should pay little attention to how people praise you and what they think about you. If we truly knew why people were praising or judging us, we would pay no heed at all.

Amassing excessive wealth can be explained only by the desire of fame. Lies can be explained only by the desire people have to seem better than they are. A person may think one thing but say another. Why? There is no other explanation than that he wants to win other people's praise.

Judgment and Punishment

Some people believe that to educate children, you must punish them. However, you can only truly educate others with a good word and by good example. Repaying evil with evil does not educate but rather spoils a person.

It is difficult to follow the lesson of nonviolence, but is it easier to follow the lesson of fighting and revenge? Millions are killed in wars. In each battle, more are killed and more suffering is endured than during the centuries of nonviolent resistance.

People say, Stop punishing, and stop returning evil for evil. Others reply, If we stop punishing evil, evil will never disappear. It is as if they are saying, If the ice on the frozen river melts, the river will disappear. But in reality if the ice melted, the boats and ships could move along the waters, and a new life would begin.

Soul

Scholars were digging in an ancient burial ground and found several kernels of wheat, which they planted and watered. Suddenly each kernel began to understand that it was at the same time both a seed and a sprout.

We are talking about the life of the spirit after death. If the spirit can live after death, then it must have lived before birth. One-sided eternity makes no sense.

There is the beginning of life, my inner spirit, inside me. I clearly understand the limits of my body and vaguely understand the limits of the spirits of others. Still vaguer is my understanding of the spirit living in animals; yet even vaguer is my feeling for animate objects. I do not sense their spirits but feel that the beginning of the world that gives life to all of us exists everywhere.

Soul

If a person does not feel the power of God within, this does not mean that the power of God does not abide in him, simply that he has not learned how to understand it.

We should learn how to love in the same way people learn how to play the violin.

Jesus Christ tried to improve the inner person. This is the opposite of what the Pharisees were doing, taking care only of appearances.

All people wash their hands before eating and clean their cookware, but they forget about cleansing their souls.

Your heart is neglected, and filled with sin and temptations. Jesus said that you should go into your heart and pull out every bad weed. The outer things are not as necessary as the inner things. True good or bad happens within you.

— FÉLICITÉ ROBERT DE LAMENNAIS

Faith

When a person studies God's law but doesn't show another how to follow it, it reminds me of a farmer who plows his soil but fails to plant his seeds.

Christ taught that out of all things we are doing, there is only one that brings true love and happiness — loving each other.

To accept ancient religious legends as undeniable truth can be a source of suffering for many people.

The person who drinks from a muddy, dirty pool in the street when there is a wonderful spring of fresh water available in his own home is stupid.   — ANGELUS SILESIUS

False Science

The difference between material and spiritual poison is that material poison tastes bad when you try it, but spiritual poison, in the form of bad newspapers or books, often looks attractive to us.

The development of science does not necessarily improve the development of our morality.

Science can make truly great progress in the study of the material world. But in the study of the inner spiritual world, science is not only unnecessary but can lead you to make wrong decisions.

Scholarly life, education, and science can turn into leaves on the tree of your life, and still not bring any fruit. — GEORGE C. LICHTENBERG

Effort

 Deep inside of you, there is a source of goodness. It is like a well that flows better when you keep it clean and keep digging deeper.

As you make progress in your spiritual life, you will see some negative things in yourself that you hadn't noticed before. This does not mean you are worse than before but that you are becoming better as you improve yourself.

If we destroyed one sin, ten others would disappear.

The person who suffers to the end will be saved, says the scripture. Often a person becomes desperate, stops, and even turns back when only a little more effort is needed to reach his goal.

Self-Sacrifice

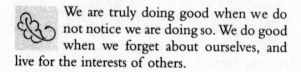 We are truly doing good when we do not notice we are doing so. We do good when we forget about ourselves, and live for the interests of others.

Loving yourself is a necessary aspect of a good life. It is a very strong feeling in your childhood but should grow weaker as you advance in years.

It is impossible for a person who lies to himself to live a life dedicated to others. For the person who is already living for others, it is impossible to imagine he could live his life for only himself.

A person can deny his own life only for a truly God-filled life. All other types of self-denial are mistakes.

Humility

When you feel unhappy, think of all the bad things that you have done. This may make you feel worse, but it should force you to start improving yourself.

It does not matter how much our individual lives differ, the distance from humanity to perfection is the same for everyone, since we are all equally far from achieving it.

Some people try to position themselves as teachers over others, but often they should be the students.

If you are seeking someone to be a role model for your life, try to find a simple and humble person. Only among such people can be found true greatness.

Truth

 To understand how to be truthful toward others, be truthful to yourself.

It makes sense to say truthfulness is the greatest virtue. We can say with certainty that, without truthfulness, no other virtue can exist.

If a chicken in its egg had a human's sophisticated mind and could use it as an educated person does, it would never break its shell, and would fail to get out and know the real truth.

To feed the hungry, clothe the naked, and visit and comfort the sick are all good things, but there is one more besides these: to help others get rid of their prejudices, mistakes, and erroneous views about life.

Thoughts

It is better to do more than less, better to arrive early than late. The reproaches of your conscience may be more painful for those things you have done than for what remains to be done.

Every time you want to speak, stop and think: Is what you want to say worth saying?

If you cannot restrain your bodily desires now, it may be that you could have stopped them once when the desire was only a passing thought that you failed to bring under control at the time.

When you feel depressed, or in a bad mood, think of yourself as being sick. Do not move too much, do not do anything, just wait until you are feeling better.

Words

 Nothing supports idleness as much as empty talk.

If one word is worth a coin, then silence is worth two. If silence sits well with those who are clever, then it should sit even better with those who are stupid. — THE TALMUD

Those who criticize me behind my back are afraid of me; those who praise me to my face hate me. — CHINESE PROVERB

Words are great things. You can unite people with words or separate them; you can create love or animosity.

Two things can reveal faulty thinking: to be silent when you need to speak, or to speak when you should be silent.

Thoughts

 A person's fate follows his train of thought. A person can visualize and create his life with his thoughts.

Our thoughts, good or bad, send us to either hell or paradise. This happens not in heaven or hell, but in our present life.

A true prayer is crucial to your spirit, because when you talk to God directly, your intellect can attain its highest level of ability.

When you seek truth, your life begins. When you stop looking for truth, your life ends.

Our life and thoughts are the same. Life is born in our hearts and formed by our thoughts. If one speaks and acts with good thoughts, then joy will follow like a shadow that never leaves.

— BUDDHIST PROVERB

269

There Is No Evil

We have two kinds of problems in our lives. The first are solvable problems, where we have to make every effort to resolve them. The second are those we cannot solve or overcome; we need the patience to live with them and still keep improving ourselves.

You may worry about many things: your lack of money, illness, humiliation, and libel. But as soon as you pity yourself, you feel miserable. When you try to make the best you can of any situation instead of feeling desperate, you will feel confident and energetic about your life.

When you are not satisfied in your life, be like a snail and retreat into your shell. Wait until the circumstance disappears; your life will change for the better, and you can go on.

We often say that suffering is evil. But if there were no suffering, we would not know our limits.

Living in the Present

A wise man was once asked, "What is the most important time in your life?" He answered, "The present moment, because you are the master of your life only in the present."

Our actions in this particular moment belong to us. What will become of them belongs to God. — FRANCIS OF ASSISI

Do not make great plans, or think too much about what will result from your efforts, which seem to me as the efforts of an ant or a tiny insect. All you have to do is live your life, avoid the bad, and try to do only what is good.

We should desire only things done in the present. Desiring something from your past is to feel sorry for yourself; desires for the future are visions and daydreams. Concentrating on your present desires — this is real life.

Death

 If life is good, then death too is good; for without death, there can be no life.

Death is destruction of those organs that connect you to the world, and thus, questions about your future life have no sense in connection to death.

We should not think about death too much, but only live our lives and keep death in mind. When you can do so, life becomes a truly serious, fruitful, and joyful thing.

The fear of death is in direct opposition to a godly life. If you are living a truly godly life, this fear will come close to zero.

After Death

 For faith, you need to believe that your life is eternal, and live accordingly.

Nothing can better help you meet death with quiet assurance than the belief that death is a transformation to another, better state where we existed before our birth.

A person who is dying can in those moments barely understand what is going on around him. This happens not because he does not understand this world anymore, but because he understands something different — the things in life that those around him cannot understand. Something completely other attracts his attention.

If we believe that all that has happened to us in this life was for our own good, then all that will happen to us after we die will be for our own good as well.

Happiness

If there is a kind God, a God of love, He most definitely created things so that all people would feel good in the long run. To feel good, we should love one another. And since God is love, sooner or later we will all come to God.

Happiness does not depend on heaven or earth. Happiness is inside of us. What is happiness? Living a life filled with love makes it very easy for us to be happy.

The will of God will be fulfilled anyway, whether I want it to or not. Therefore, we should live in love and feel good for our own sakes.

For there to be goodness for all, we need to be at our best in the family. To be at your best in the family, you need to be your best individually. To be your best individually, you need to have inner goodness. To have inner goodness, you need to have goodness in your heart. To have goodness in your heart, you need to have good thoughts.

Faith

 The essence of every religion is its answer to the same questions, "Why do I live, and what is my attitude and relationship with the world around me?"

The nonreligious person with no preconceived attitude to this world is as impossible as a man without a heart.

Every person should develop his or her view of the world. You can make use of the old traditions and beliefs, but you should test them against your own intellect and logic.

Religion is that state of mind in which your actions are driven not by the things of this temporary life but rather by the things of eternal, limitless life.

Soul

You cannot understand God only with your mind. You know He exists, not just with your intellect but with your whole being, because you can feel His spirit living inside you.

Those who do not accept the belief in our spiritual origin base their actions on connections between material things and objects. This connection is so complicated you can never understand it, because every action has a consequence, and every consequence leads to numerous others.

True life is found in understanding the basis of your spiritual origin.

The voice of your passions can be louder than that of your conscience. Your passions speak differently — they scream at you — whereas your conscience speaks to you in a quiet but firm voice.   — WILLIAM ELLERY CHANNING

One Soul in All

 God lives in everyone, and everyone lives in God. Those who understand this cannot treat any living being with contempt.

I remember when I was young, I used to shoot birds and animals while I was hunting. When I think how I would kill those gravely wounded creatures by stabbing my knife into their hearts, I remember with horror.

The eye that too often looks closely at the material world grows blind, and loses its ability to see oneself and God.

You should respect all people, but you should have one hundred times more respect for a child than any adult, so that you do not damage the purity of a child's spirit.

God

 The more you forget yourself, the more God will enter inside of you.

Why do we need the sun, spring, winter? Why do we need lives filled with joy and sufferings that end in death? Why do we need so much energy in our lives? All this proves to me that we are living for a specific intelligent and kind reason, though I may not understand the cause.

Should we prove the existence of God? Can anything be more stupid? Proving His existence means you need to prove your own existence. To whom? Why? If God does not exist, then nothing exists.

I fill all space and all time, and I am in the heart of every person.

A human being must love someone, and we can only truly love one thing — that which is pure. And there is only one such being — that is God.

Unification in Spirit

If a person lives only for his body, it is as if he has closed himself in a prison. The person who lives for his spirit opens his prison doors, and sets himself free.

Do not ignore your conscience, but listen to it. It will lead you toward the truth you need.

Why do I feel so angry when I have a disagreement with someone? Why do I feel so embarrassed when I don't love a particular person? When we do not love others, and we disagree with them, we are disagreeing with God, who lives in us all. We are essentially disagreeing with ourselves.

For God, I am a different person than I am for myself. God brings out the best in me.

Universal Love

 Fight the sin, but make peace with the sinner. Hate the bad things a person does, but not the person.

The soft and tender roots of a plant can make their way though the hardest soil, even the cracks in a rock. Love works in the same way; nothing can resist love. — HENRY DAVID THOREAU

Loving your neighbor without loving God is like a plant having no roots.

When you love your neighbor because you love God, you have to love everyone, even those who dislike you or who are ugly. The only love that is good never dies or ebbs away.

Sin

Very often a person wearing clean, shiny new shoes will walk carefully around the mud, then make a misstep and go into it as if he wasn't careful. When he sees his shoes have muck all over them, he will keep heading straight through the mud and get filthier and filthier. Do not do this in your spiritual life. If you venture into filth, get out of it, and clean yourself.

A small sin can lead to a bigger sin.

Buddhists believe there are five major sins: murder, theft, lust, lying, and drinking alcohol. The following are ways to fight these sins: restrictions, humble living, hard work, humility, and faith.

Even the goodness that comes to people who are deep in sin, prejudice, and error can seem evil to them.

Sin

 The sins of the body are commonplace and frequent, and there is no one who does not sin in this way. We spend all our life seeking freedom from them.

There is a trinity of curses — drunkenness, eating meat, and smoking. If we did not have to deal with these, our lives would be completely different.

You can please your body with wealth, but the more you please it, the more it needs. There is no wealth great enough to please all your bodily desires.

The sin of serving your body can be manifested in many ways. One of the most common and customary ways is to eat to excess.

Work and Idleness

 Work makes you noble. A lazy, idle person cannot be respected.

Not having a good work ethic is worse than all misfortunes. Children should start developing this necessary habit from their early childhood years.

It is not enough to be a hardworking person. Equally important is the job you are working at.
— HENRY DAVID THOREAU

Nature does not take breaks in its development, and punishes all idleness.

A very important condition of happiness is work. First, work you like to do. Second, physical work you do with your body that gives you good sleep and much happiness.

Desire and Passion

For a person to be celibate is good, if you can afford it. If you cannot be celibate, then you should live in an honest marriage, and together with your spouse raise your children.

Some nations with a rudimentary social system practice polygamy. Yet they do not practice the sexual immorality that comes with marrying and divorcing many times over in the pretext of monogamy that exists among the peoples of the Christian world.

People in our world think that church marriage frees them from the requirements of celibacy and purity in sex, giving them permission to have sexual relationships without restriction.

The passions caused by sexual attraction seem like tiny shining lights above a swamp. They lure us into the bog, and then disappear.

— ARTHUR SCHOPENHAUER

Judgment and Punishment

 If someone is guilty of doing something bad to you, you can respond in two ways. First, you can seek revenge and feel cold and hard. Second, you can forgive and feel joy. Which would you rather do?

Be careful if you want to strike the devil in another person but fail to notice the presence of God in them.

If you judge others, do not forget that they have the spirit of God in them.

When I recall my previous life, I clearly see that I never fought with those in a higher class than me. However, the slightest wrong by someone of a lower class made me angry.

What can be done when a person is angry at you and harms you? You can do many things, but should not do this — respond with evil to the evil done to you.

Pride

 The joy of a wise and kind person lies in his conscience, not on the lips of others.

A person is proud of the superficial rewards of this world, thinking they elevate him above others. He does not recognize that the inner growth and inner merits of his spirit are more important than all other awards and medals, which are like the small light of a candle in bright sunlight.

Family can be the reason, but not the excuse, for bad actions.

Pride may increase or decrease according to your material success, but it does not improve your dignity.

Remember that the purpose of our lives is the unification of people, and any attempts to be better or more important than others will separate you from this goal.

Effort

 What is real power? If you shape iron, amass a lot of money, or conquer another nation with your soldiers, this is not real power. Real power is displayed when you forgive those who treat you with evil. For then you are stronger than anyone, because the power of God will be with you.

One of the most dangerous and unpleasant phrases for me is: "Everything is all right."

We are ready to behave as cowards so that others will consider us brave.

Neither praise nor judge yourself before others. Mind the voice of your conscience and not the judgments of others.

I am sad because I will not see the results of my life's efforts in this world.

Greed and Wealth

 People like to say: This is my house, my property, my child, my money. They do not understand how a person who is seeking God can believe that all things belong to God. — THE TALMUD

Thinking that enormous wealth makes your life easier is the same as thinking that it is easier to walk while carrying a burden.

Wealth is relative. By itself, it means nothing, like a numerator without a denominator in a fraction. A person cannot be completely unhappy not having things that he never even thought about yesterday. Someone who has too many possessions keeps himself unhappy and busy with things that he really does not need.
— ARTHUR SCHOPENHAUER

Judgment and Punishment

 Fear of future punishment has never stopped a murderer.

Many years will pass, and our great-grandchildren will talk about our prisons, courts, and executions in the same way that we look at burning people on the stake during medieval times, saying, "How could they not see the senselessness and evil of what they were doing?"

There is no law in nature that can force a person to do evil to his neighbor, just as there is no law in nature that can force a person to become an alcoholic.

Trees can be shaped and molded by man for a period of time but will still grow in the same way they were designed to. We should remember this when we are punishing our children for wrongdoings, because their nature will prevail, and they will grow up according to their potential anyway.

Violence and War

 People make a great mistake thinking that freedom, equality, and brotherhood can be introduced by capital punishment and violence.

If the law of God does not coincide with the law of men, which law should we listen to? The law of God says, "All are brothers"; the law of men says, "Kill your enemies."

People often do completely stupid and cruel things and tell lies when they come to power. This does not happen by chance but is a general rule, a necessary requirement of people in power.

If you want to be set free from the power of people, you should seek the power of God. If you feel protected by God, then people cannot do anything to you.

Love

 An old Chinese man said that to climb a tall mountain, you need to make the first small step. This small task is a practical teaching of unification and love.

You can believe that your thoughts are not working properly because your brain isn't getting enough blood. You can also believe that your bad mood is because your liver is not functioning properly. But maybe it is the contrary — because of your bad thoughts, there is not enough blood circulation, and due to your bad mood, your liver does not work properly. What is the cause and what is the consequence here?

All the famous commandments use the negation "do not" — such as Do not steal, Do not kill, and so on. Positive commandments can be applied to our inner spiritual activity — you should love; you should do to your neighbor as you want to be done to you, and so forth.

Faith

 True faith is the knowledge not of what was or what will be, but of what is, more specifically, what a person should do at this present moment.

In our time, most people only imagine that they are preaching Christianity. In reality, they are following the morals of the pagan world.

If you do not free yourself from prejudice, you cannot face God directly. You should read the teachings of God not in the Bible, but in your heart.

There are false teachers who ask people to live a good life by scaring them with the possibility of future punishment. As a reward, these teachers promise a better world — a world in which they have never lived.

False Science

 Never be ashamed to ask the things you do not know.

A scholarly person is one who has read many books; an educated person is one who knows what is popular among people. Do not try to be scholarly or educated, but be yourself.

Do not be afraid of a lack of education; do not be afraid of hesitations. Instead, be afraid of this: pretending to know what you do not know.

Math, physics, chemistry, and all other sciences develop only one particular side of this life, and do not make any conclusions about this life in general.

Effort

 Nothing can weaken a person more than the belief that something other than his own effort is needed to find goodness.

Life without moral effort and self-improvement is a dream.

What I should do is within my power, what happens to me is not. Whatever happens, it can only help me to do good.

If someone agrees that his life is not good enough, he can try to change his outer conditions, to change his life for the better. However, first of all, you need to change your inner spirit. This you can do anywhere, at any time.

Self-Sacrifice

 Being firm with yourself in sexual matters is a clear sign of your serious attitude toward moral issues in general.

It can be difficult for a young person to deny the joys of his youth. We should teach them that the more they deny their material life, the greater the goodness they will receive in their spiritual life.

Denying your body's material pleasures will give your soul the same joy as the physical satisfaction that pleasure gives to your body.

What you give away belongs to you; what you keep belongs not only to you but also to others. If you gave something to others, you did something good for yourself. It will stay with you forever, and no one can take it away from you. If you keep something, you keep it only until the moment when you will have to give it away, and you will have to give it away when you die.

Humility

We do not know, and cannot know, the purpose of why we are alive, or why we came into this world. But if we know what the force that put us in this world wants, then we can do it well. The best thing we can do is to increase love in others.

Nothing is softer or more yielding than water, yet nothing can beat it for strength. The weak defeats the strong, tenderness defeats cruelty, humility defeats pride. Everyone knows this law, but nobody follows it.

It is difficult for anyone to love those who are overly confident, proud, and boastful. This shows the importance of living with humility and meekness. These qualities arouse love — the most important thing among people.

Truth

Do not think it easy to tell the truth. When you are by yourself, you know the truth, but when you begin talking to others, trying to please them, your words get tangled, and you start telling lies. Beware of this.

We like truth more than lies, but when it comes to our lives, we choose lies over truth.

Truth by itself is neither a vice nor a virtue, but it is an essential part of everything that is good.

There are lies spoken on purpose, when a person knows it is a lie, and speaks it for his own benefit. There are also involuntary lies, when a person does not know how to speak the truth.

Effort

If one person achieves thousands of victories over thousands of people in battle, and another achieves a victory over himself, the latter has the more important victory.

The more I live, the more I understand the wisdom in doing nothing. It is said to work even with wild animals — they do not touch you if you lie down and stay motionless. It also works in dealing with angry people. When they see you silent and motionless, they feel the silence of God when He is observing evil.

The real force of a person is not found in active physical work but in complete inner balance and calm.

The more you hurry, the less you will get done.

Words

You may regret one time out of a hundred that you did not say what you were supposed to say. But you will regret ninety-nine times out of a hundred that you spoke instead of keeping silent.

Two things are wrong — silence when you were meant to speak, and speaking when you were meant to stay silent.

Often silence is the wisest of answers. Let your tongue relax more often than your hands. Silence is the best response to an ignorant and rude person.

If your tongue is good, there is nothing better. If your tongue is bad, there is nothing worse.
— THE TALMUD

Thoughts

 The bad thought that precedes an evil deed is worse than the act itself. You can repent of a bad act and not repeat it. But a bad thought may lead to more bad actions.

The decision to transfer the focus of our life from the physical to the spiritual is made by conscious thought.

Any person can be wise, whether young or old, clever or stupid, educated or not.

Wisdom is important for all and can be achieved if you follow the law of God, which we know in our conscience. It is more important than any personal desire.

Great thoughts come from the heart.
— LUC DE CLAPIERS,
MARQUIS DE VAUVENARGUES

Living in the Present

 What happens to us has so many consequences, causes, and reasons that if we
were to go deeper, the human brain
would be powerless to explain it. We do not
know the future, and it cannot be revealed to us.
What then can we do? Live only in the present.
It is all that truly belongs to us.

You cannot believe in a future life. There is
life only in the present, and the present cannot
disappear.

God is not limited to space and time. He is
beyond space and time.

This divine, spiritual part of me is manifested in the present. Thus, I think my true life
is in this present moment.

There Is No Evil

You ask me the question, "Why does evil exist here in this world?" I reply with another question, "Why does life exist?" Evil exists because life exists. Life reveals itself in eradicating evil.

Everything can be saved in the moment you think all is lost.

Everything is done for good: illness, poverty, shame, or other troubles. Only these reveal our spiritual foundations to us.

When we are the weakest in our bodies, we are the strongest in our spirit.

Evil is goodness that is not properly understood.

Death

Everyone is positive that sooner or later death will come for us all. We can prepare for bed, for tomorrow, for the coming winter, so why do we not prepare for death? The best way to do so is to live a good life. The better you live your life, the less you will fear death. There is no fear of death for a saint.

Just as a burning candle melts the wax, the life of our spirit destroys our body. Our body burns from the fire in our spirit, and burns away completely when death comes.

The fear of death is not natural to the intellectual being. The fear of death is the understanding of your sin.

A person who is afraid of death is one who has not lived his life properly and has broken the law of life.

After Death

The longer a person lives, the more his life will be revealed to him. The unknown becomes known, and this happens until death. At the moment of death, everything is revealed, and we can understand all about this life.

Death is a change in our body, the biggest, and the last, change.

We do not know what happens after the final change. No one tells us that a person who goes away and fails to write does not exist. We just know that we do not receive news from him. The same happens with the people who die.

I just saw a person pass by my window. I saw him for a second in my window, but I knew he was walking before, and still will be walking after, this moment.

Happiness

A wise man once said, "I have traveled all over the world looking for goodness. Day and night, I looked for it. One day, when I was completely desperate in my search, my inner voice said, 'Goodness is within you.' I listened to this voice and found complete happiness."

Joy in life is a quality found in animals, children, and saints. Animals, because they have no human intellect and live naturally; children, because their intellect is pure and not spoiled; and saints, because life gives a saint the only thing he wants — the ability to obtain perfection, drawing closer and uniting with God.

If you do not understand the meaning of life, then you are one of many busy people who are pursuing their own lives and minding their own business, who appear neither comical or tragic but rather stupid and pitiful.

Faith

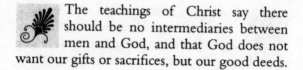 The teachings of Christ say there should be no intermediaries between men and God, and that God does not want our gifts or sacrifices, but our good deeds.

Buddha said that a person who places religion first in his life is like a man who brings a lamp into a dark house. The darkness disappears, and the light comes in. When you persist in looking for truth, you will achieve enlightenment.

We should not stop with the religious understanding that has been revealed to us already. We should not just stare at the light but use it to reveal new sides of the truth.

We know there are things around us because we have our senses — sight, hearing, touch. Those without these senses do not feel the world about them. In the same way, the person who does not feel the spirituality of his "me" cannot feel God.

Soul

 Your spirit is like a glass. God is the light shining through this glass. Your body is both a glass and the light that shines through it.

We have measured the earth, the stars, and the depths of the seas; we have discovered riverbeds and mountains on the moon. We have built clever machines, and every day we discover something new. Oh, my God, we know so many things, and we can do so much! But something, some most important thing, is missing, and we do not know exactly what. We feel bad because we know lots of unnecessary things but do not know the most important — ourselves. If only we could remember the spirit living within us, our lives would be completely different.

Life is found not in our body, but in the spirit that exists everywhere.

One Soul in All

 All people are the children of one God, so we are all brothers and sisters.

How can I be united with all people? There are so many, all so very different. How can I be one with them all? There is only one way — to become one with the spirit living in all of us, in them as well as me.

Life suddenly becomes very simple when people set as their main task not their numerous individual goals, but the one major goal — helping one another, and living by the spirit that unites us all.

If you feel bad, feel that there is nowhere to hide and you want to keep your life to yourself, then you must turn to the spiritual source within you — that is the best thing to do in such a circumstance.

God

You can love God and understand His presence as soon as you grasp the fact that the material world is just an illusion, and only temporary.

For me, God is all I strive for. God shows me the direction to move in, and all my life is in this movement. If I could understand Him completely, there would be nothing to move toward, and no point in living this life.

"Why do you ask My name?" God asked Moses. "My name is the same as My existence. I am what I am, and those who want to know my exact name do not know Me."

When there is no sun, you can see limitless stars in the sky. You are certain they exist. When the sun rises, you can no longer see them. In the same way, you cannot see God when you are blinded by the temptations of the world. Yet you know God exists, and He will reveal Himself in you.

Unification in Spirit

Unity between individuals or whole nations cannot be achieved with talk but by striving toward understanding the truth, and applying it to life. Truth unites people.

We feel bored without company, without other people in our lives. This occurs because we feel — in spite of the fact that our bodies are separate — that there is something we want to be united with in others.

The wise and the saintly who lived in this world taught people the same lesson. This lesson is simple: we all have the same spirit inside of us, and we can all be united by love.

If a person is true to himself, he will never be satisfied. He needs to be united with others and will pursue this his entire life, and from this will come spiritual growth.

Anger and Hatred

 Only one thing is necessary: we should all have a pure heart, with no anger, hatred, irritation, or hostility in it.

If you feel hostility toward another person, think about their inner state. Do not think about yourself, or that you want to prove yourself right.

In your quiet, inner thoughts, try to find the good in others. Do not say anything bad about others, even in your own thoughts. When you interact with a person, try to find as much common ground as possible, the more the better, and try to nurture this feeling.

To cease being angry with a person and instead to seek peace, forgiveness, and love toward him, remind yourself of any sins you may have in common and compare them.

Pride

 Every person, when inwardly focused on himself, thinks his own life to be the only true life and the lives of others to be unimportant. If each person thinks his own life is more important than those of others, then everybody's lives are equal.

Weeds, when they get into a wheat field, sap water from the soil, block the sunshine, and tarnish the good wheat. The same happens with pride in a person. It takes his power and closes him off from the light of the truth.

The more prideful a person is, the more those who use him will think him stupid and try to abuse or manipulate him. Pride always goes hand in hand with stupidity.

Vanity and Fame

 When educating children, among the first things they should be taught is that their actions should not depend on the opinions of others.

Every good deed holds the desire for fame, support, or the praise of other people, and this in itself is not bad. What is bad is when the deed is done for fame only.

Our major problems do not come from a few truly bad people but from the huge crowd surrounding us that pulls us all in the same direction, just like a current.

Vanity and seeking fame are the last garments you will have to take off. They are difficult to remove, because they prevent your spirit from being free.

Judgment and Punishment

 Repay evil with goodness, and forgive everyone. Only when we all live this way will evil disappear.

Very often, there are those who disagree with Christ's teaching to repay goodness for an evil done to you. They say if we follow this rule, the existing order of the world will be destroyed. But this lesson was taught to the world in order to destroy the old, bad order and to create a new, good, Christlike order.

Clearly, different people define evil in different ways. What Peter thinks is good, Ivan will see as bad. If Peter responds to this belief of Ivan's with evil, evil will continue to grow. Therefore, we should respond only with goodness.

Violence and War

Why is it easy to manage other people's lives and to tell others what to do? People do this because if they make the wrong decisions, they themselves will not be the ones to suffer.

The person telling others what to do with their lives does not have time to live his own.

Some people force others to live their lives according to their imposed views and then try to find justifications for the violence required to impose them.

People pay most of their attention to the outer forms of their relationships, to rituals and how people behave. Forms are not important. True life is found in relating to people.

Violence and War

 From any viewpoint, if violence were to cease in this world, everyone's life would be improved.

Christianity teaches us to follow the will of Christ and no other; evil opposes this will.

Human freedom, morality, and dignity are based on the premise that a person performs good deeds not because he is forced to, but because of his inner voice.

Can anything be more stupid than the statement that a man living on the other side of the river has a right to kill me simply because the ruler of his country is in a quarrel with the ruler of my country?

You cannot rule and remain innocent.

Faith

 True faith does not need the institution of the official church. That institution is slavery.

The more illogical and harmful the institution, the more artificial greatness, glitter, and pomposity it has; otherwise it could not attract people. This is the official institution of the church.

It is terrible to think that the great, necessary, and simple teachings of Christianity were changed by the official church into a rude persuasion and hypnosis appealing to the lower characteristics of the human spirit.

Our belief in miracles comes from our pride. We think we are such important creatures that, for our sake, God changed the flow of this life.

False Science

 Study not to become a scholar but so you can live a better life.

A person is given intellect so he can discern the meaning of life — how to live a good life and how not to enter bad paths.

Divine truth is often revealed to us in the speech of the uneducated or a child, not in the harmful and erroneous thoughts scholars write in their books.

Writers and novelists are from the same mold as the rest of us in life. Most people are either stupid or mistaken. As a result, there are too many bad books, which become a complete waste of time, money, and attention. Bad books are not only useless, they are harmful. Nine out of every ten are published only to lure money from our pockets. Therefore, it is best not to read the books that are the most popular. First try to read and study the best writers of all times and nations, for only these authors teach and educate us.

Effort

 A good effort is good only when it is repeated. When you fall, keep getting up again; do not fall into despair when you have to repeat your efforts.

A silkworm should be your example. It works until the time it can become a butterfly and fly. If you work on improving your spirit, you will find your own wings.

You will never see the end result of your efforts, because no matter how far you go, perfection still eludes you. The effort is not the tool for reaching goodness, but is goodness in itself.

I am the tool that God is using. To achieve your purpose, you should keep your tool, your inner spirit, in order, both clean and sharp.

Self-Sacrifice

 I do not like my life. I feel as if I am deeply immersed in sin; as soon as I become free of one, I fall into another. How can I improve my life? But in fact, it used to be even worse, for I used to live only for the sake of my body. My life is getting better, because I am trying to improve my spirit.

The highest goodness, happiness, or freedom a person can achieve is in denying yourself for the sake of love.

The longer you live, the more you realize that you will not get all you want from life, and your life could end at any moment. Then you begin to understand there is no real life in your body, and when you've reached this understanding, you stop living for your body and concentrate on the spirit of God.

Humility

 The less satisfied a person is with himself, the more useful he will be to others.

Everyone knows something about himself that is worse than what his neighbor has done. If you keep this in mind, humility becomes easy.

Try to see your real potential. If you know it, do not boast about it to others.

You should not forget your own sins, for then it will be easier to forgive the sins of others.

There is always a dark spot in any sunlight. It is the shadow of my self-respect.

Truth

If our life contradicts nature, it is better to accept the truth than to hide it. We can change our life according to the truth, but we cannot change the truth.

When we look at someone's work, it seems to us that if we tried, we could do the same. When you see a person who is telling the truth, we think we can do the same, but it is not as easy as it looks.

Living with a lie is sometimes easier and more convenient than telling the truth, but it is difficult to stop lying. When you tell the truth, you do not have to say anything else. When you lie, you have to keep on lying to justify your previous lies.

Effort

 If you have to choose between keeping busy all day with useless activity and empty conversation or doing nothing, then it is better to do nothing than to do vacuous, harmful things.

There is nothing more important for your inner growth than to abstain from wrongdoing. It can become a habit, and can bring you real virtue.

Miracles are necessary when people have no intellectual basis for their faith.

A good horseman uses the reins to control the horse, not just to hang on. In the same way, a good person not only knows anger is bad, but uses all his power to rein it in.

Words

 If you help others to eliminate their sins, God will help you twice as much to eliminate yours.

If you know the truth, or think you do, present it simply, in such a way that it will not contradict other people's views.

Our actions, both good and bad, are like children. They live and act not according to our will but to their own lives. If you commit a good or evil deed, it speeds away from you much further than you think.

The more you talk, the less you will work.

The real power of a person is found not in his busy schedule or loud actions but in his quiet, constant desire to do what is good, as expressed in his thoughts, words, and actions.

Thoughts

A person has the freedom to choose among many actions, to move to the right, to the left, or stay in one place. The more complicated choices are those that guide your emotions, such as whether to stay angry or abstain from anger. The most difficult choice in expressing your freedom is giving a proper direction to your thought.

Depression is the state of your spirit when you do not see any meaning in your life, or in the world. There is only one real remedy: find your own good thoughts and those of others that will explain what you should do with your life.

In prayer, you receive the greatest truth that can be revealed to you.

Christ said, when you pray, pray by yourself. Only then will God listen to you. God is inside of you, but for Him to be able to hear you, you need to remove anything that conceals Him from you.

There Is No Evil

 If you feel yourself sick and weak, re-member that if you are unable to do anything good, you should avoid doing bad things.

Evil is the field being plowed by goodness, the wood burned in the fire of goodness, the candle lit by the light of goodness.

All your misery and misfortunes mean nothing when you understand that the evil of this world lies only in your attitude and is within you.

Any misfortune or suffering is not as bad as the fear of facing it.

Living in the Present

 If you do something and think about the consequences, then you do it only for yourself.

The consequences of most of our actions are not revealed to us, because we live in a limited world, and consequences are without limit. If you can see all the consequences of an action, then the action was of little significance.

Just do what you are doing now, and believe this moment will be good for the hours, years, and centuries to come.

— RALPH WALDO EMERSON

What is important is not the length of your life but its depth.

It is strange how closely we are connected with this world. Yet at the same time, I understand this world to be only an illusion, that there is another, higher world and purpose.

Death

 We should begin to prepare for death not by fasting, writing our will, or saying good-bye to those we know, but by living our life in the way God wants us to. I came into this life by God's hand, and I will return to Him when my life is over.

People who do not understand what life is really about cannot truly understand death.

When we pass from one act to another, the scenery changes. What we think for a moment is reality is only theater. In the same way, at the moment of death, a person sees what really exists both here and out there, which makes the moment of death truly pivotal.

At the moment of death, a person's candle — the light by which he wrote his life filled with worries, lies, woes, and evil — this candle illuminates the surroundings with a special bright light, makes a snapping sound, and then disappears forever.

Universal Love

If you do not love people, your whole life becomes complex and difficult. If you begin to love people, everything in your life will become clear and easy.

Without love, a person feels surrounded by enemies. Love unites him with all living creatures of the world, past, present, and future, and love unites him with God.

The activity of people who do not understand the true meaning of life is always directed at the struggle of existence, acquiring more wealth and pleasures, and not at getting rid of their sufferings and preparing for eternal life. The more people are busy with this in their daily lives, the less time they will have for the only true pleasure man has, love.

One day, somehow, we will stop the fighting, wars, and executions and start loving one another. Eventually that time will come because what originally was put into our souls was not hatred for others but love. Let us do everything we can to make this time arrive as soon as possible.

Soul

It is the most critical and difficult age when a person's physical development stops. The growth of your body ceases, and your inner spiritual growth begins.

All living beings grow constantly. Our spirits grow like our children, both the spirit of one person and of all people.

There are four stages in life: (1) the "animal-like" life, which is the newborn stage; (2) "I follow others," the childhood stage; (3) "live for fame and glory," the youth stage; (4) "live for your spirit and for God," which is the true life.

Every person goes from one season of the year to another, from winter to spring. First, you have showers of water raining down, the opening of the buds, the leaves on the oak trees, and then flowers, seeds, and fruit. I feel that both within me and within mankind, the fruit will be ready soon.

Desire and Passion

When people marry but feel that they could have remained single, it is the same as a walking person falling without having stumbled. If you feel you can live without marriage, keeping a celibate life, it is better for you not to marry at all.

The most active desires that can possess us at times are our sexual desires. The more you indulge them, the bigger they will grow.

Sexual passion is a source of great suffering. Therefore, people should fight to subdue it. Yet people today try artificially to enhance this passion, treating it as a refined feeling.

Young men feel shame when they deal with sex for the first time. Remember this shame. This is the voice of God in you.

Temptation

 All that you really need can be easily achieved. All that you do not need, you can achieve only with great difficulty.

People do not need alcohol, drugs, or tobacco to live. Everyone knows these are harmful for your body and spirit. However, millions of people work in the production of these poisons. Why?

The foods that are necessary for a person to maintain his life — bread, fruit, nuts, vegetables, and water — are easy to get and do not cost much.

It is not the poor, who eat simple foods, who should envy the rich with their spoiled stomachs, but the unhealthy rich who should envy the healthy poor.

Greed and Wealth

 What a strange prejudice, that wealth brings happiness. Will people ever banish this notion?

People put a thousand times more effort into increasing their wealth than increasing their wisdom. However, we all understand that being happy is much more important than having an abundance of things. — ARTHUR SCHOPENHAUER

The person who keeps what he has without sharing what he does not need is worse than the thief who stole what he needs to survive.

Nothing is more useless than to acquire, increase, and hoard money.

Work and Idleness

 An old wise man once said, "It is better to make your own bread with your own hands than to be another man's servant. It is better to grease your hands in the clay at work, than to cross them humbly as someone's servant."

Without physical work you cannot be truly healthy, for lacking it you would have no healthy thoughts.

If you want always to be in a good mood — then regularly do physically work until you grow a little tired.

Work is a necessity, for life without work is suffering and not a virtue. Thinking of work as a virtue is similar to how we think about eating.

Anger and Hatred

 You say you are surrounded by bad people. If you really think so, you yourself must be bad.

The water in a deep river is not disturbed if you throw a stone into it. Therefore, if a person becomes troubled after rude words are spoken to him, he is not a river but instead a puddle of mud.

To be clean in your spirit is to be free. How can you be free when you are bound by your emotions, such as anger or irritation?

Those whose spirits are not free look but cannot see, listen but cannot hear, eat without really tasting the food.

Pride

 Proud people harm themselves first, because they refuse themselves the greatest pleasure — communication with others.

I can understand that people treat each other as unequal when someone is stronger, bigger, smarter, or kinder than others. In most cases, though, people are called unequal because one is well dressed and the other is clothed in rags.

When discussing inequality, there are two groups equally to blame: those who think themselves superior, and those who accept that they are inferior.

For the Christian person, family cannot be an excuse for bad behavior, as family was never preached by Christ. Family is the consequence of the animal side of a human's life, which cannot be an excuse to step away from Christ's love for everyone.

Thoughts

 The major difference between people lies in the fact that some live with their own thoughts while others live with other people's thoughts.

When people tell you, "Do as others do," in most cases this means behaving badly.

The more people believe in certain ideas, the more cautiously you should treat their points of view, and study them carefully.

The reasons for most of our misfortunes are not in our deeds, but in our thoughts.

Great thoughts do not need people's praise. They have great force and will move people, whether people want it or not.

Violence and War

 The evil from which we wish to protect ourselves is much less than the evil
we inflict on ourselves by engaging in
violent acts for our protection.

The peaceful response to violence seems
primitive, if we look at it from a pagan perspec-
tive on life; but to the Christian who believes in
the law of life, resisting evil is illogical.

We need to remember that we do not have
the power or the right to tell others what to do,
but should concern ourselves with our own lives.

No society can rid itself of evil if its people
remain as they are now.

Prayer

 Prayer cannot be the same every day. Sometimes I want help, sometimes I want to thank the Lord, and sometimes I want to remember Him.

My morning prayer: I believe that God lives in me and in every person, and therefore I want to love and glorify Him in me and every person I see. I do not want to do anything against God's will, I do not want to abuse, scold, or judge others, I want to do to others what I wish to be done to me, and I want to love all others.

My evening prayer: I believe God is in me and in other people. I do not want to do anything against Him, but I have done some things that were not good. Why did I do them, and how can I avoid doing bad things in the future?

Help me, God, not to judge people, neither in my words, nor in my thoughts.

Judgment and Punishment

What is a thief or a con man but a man who is lost? We should take pity on him and not be angry at him. Yet some say we should punish him. If a man loses his sight, we do not punish him, but pity him.

Through the use of punishment, the government creates more criminals than it punishes.

The major evil of the government is found not in the destruction of life but in the destruction of love.

You cannot fight lies with laws based on violence.

Avoid blaming others, and you will feel a joy similar to what an alcoholic feels when he stops drinking. This is the beautiful joy of being pure.

Faith

 Faith is a set of established attitudes toward God and the world. What happens to the life of those with faulty foundations to their faith?

From the beginning of Christianity, the first Christians did not fully understand the teachings of Christ. They taught about the resurrection, miracles, and the coming of Holy Spirit but spoke little about the moral and practical side of Christianity, that is, love.

Real truth is not in believing miracles but in understanding the truth.

A person who believes in miracles and that Christ will come to judge the living and the dead — this person does not necessarily believe in the God of love and in the brotherhood of all people.

Truth

No one is completely truthful and without deceit. The only difference between a truthful person and a liar is that the one strives to tell the truth, while the other does not.

True knowledge humbles the great, amazes the masses, and elevates the small.

We should always live, think, and speak the truth. Yes, we should always speak the truth, not only in big things but also in the small details of everyday life. Do not tarnish yourself with lies.

Calling your limited knowledge of this world "science" does not make it more important. What is truly important is what is good for us all.

The primary purpose of your intellect is to reveal the truth, and any attempt to hide the truth is one of your intellect's major errors.

Effort

 Everything good, even the smallest good act, takes effort.

Nothing can stop you from making an effort to improve your life. Always remember this.

We think of work as the things we can see with our eyes: building houses, plowing fields, feeding cattle. However, your only true work is invisible: it is improving your inner spirit.

To live a good life, do not neglect even the smallest good act. Such acts require the same amount of energy as the greatest deeds and the most important actions.

Self-Sacrifice

To deny yourself is to deny what belongs to you. If I am ready for self-denial, I understand my divine part and am ready for eternity. The divine spirit inside of me will have to deny the material world.

There is one law for every individual and for all people. It says, "To improve your life, you should be ready to give it away."

Real life starts when true self-denial begins.

The understanding that I can do it because I have to do it opens many divine gifts and blessings for a man.
— IMMANUEL KANT

Humility

 Try to draw close to those who judge you, and stay away from those who praise you. — THE TALMUD

As water does not stay on the mountain-tops, humility and meekness do not stay with the proud. They both need lower places.
— PERSIAN PROVERB

Nothing can help you to improve yourself as much as seeing your mistakes in others.

To learn humility, try to fight your proud thoughts when you are on your own.

Truth

 Do not neglect the truth, even in the smallest of things. It is not important how you speak or what people think about it, but what you say, for what you speak should be the truth.

Intellect is given to people to help them distinguish between lies and truth. As soon as you rid yourself of lies, you will know what you should about life.

Sometimes I am surprised when people defend certain illogical statements about religion, science, or politics. When I look closely, I notice people are simply defending their own position in society, doing so out of individual interest.

If an act is justified by someone for a complex reason, then you know it is a bad act. The decisions of your conscience are always simple and direct.

Actions

There are no great deeds in the world. You have simply to fulfill your duty, to do what you have to do. It is the same as if a horseman, or a farmer in a field cutting hay, said he did a great deed by cleaning out the barn, or mowing the hay.

Good actions are those that only God will know about.

In most cases, we regret not what we have done but that we have done it incorrectly.

If only people would refrain from doing what they know is wrong — killing, stealing, cheating on their spouses, telling lies, and blaming others — then the kingdom of God could easily come to us.

Words

 The best drink in the world is when a person has a rude word on his tongue, yet does not spit it out but swallows it.
— MUHAMMAD

You should learn how and when to speak, but more importantly, how and when to be silent. Very often, you regret saying something wrong, but you never regret staying silent.

The more you desire to speak, the greater the danger you will say something you shouldn't.

You should train your tongue to repeat the words, "I do not know."

People like to judge others, because it amuses their peers to listen.

Thoughts

 Strive to keep your thoughts pure. If we had no bad thoughts, we would do no bad deeds. — CONFUCIUS

The thought came to me that someone was bad, and I couldn't stop thinking about it. Then I understood that judging others is wrong, and I stopped judging them even in my thoughts.

Meditation and thought is the path to eternity; talking too much is one path to death. Those who meditate and spend much time thinking never die; those who do not have faith and speak and many empty words — they look dead.
— BUDDHIST PROVERB

It is hard to fight your passions in the midst of everyday life. You should set goals and make your plans when you are alone, and feel no passion or temptation. Then you will be able to fight your temptations in the future.

There Is No Evil

 Do not ask, "Why does evil exists in this world?" Evil comes only from within you.

People often say, in an insincere way, that suffering is sent to us by God. In reality, we don't believe this phrase anymore. Yet it is a very clear and undoubtable truth. If we endured suffering as real Christians, then our lives would become more powerful, joyful, and filled with meaning.

When people who are sad, depressed, or irritated revel in their state, this reminds me of a person sitting on a horse galloping down a steep hill; instead of trying to stop it, he lets go of the reins, and whips the horse to make it run even faster.

Everything is good. There is no evil. It only seems to you, living in time, that evil exists. There is no evil outside of time.

Living in the Present

 Time exists behind and ahead of us; but in the present moment, there is no time.

The reward for a good life, and good life in itself, exist in the present, outside of time. If you do good, then it is good now. You do not know what the consequences may be — good or bad — in the future.

You are a day laborer. You should work every day, and be paid every day.　　— THE TALMUD

Real and good life happens only when you address what you need to do to improve your spirit at this moment. The best thing to do is what unites you to others and God.

Death/After Death

Every person knows he will die, and that he comes closer to death every day. Therefore, it is enough to know that the meaning of life is independent from the flow of time to be closer to spiritual improvement.

You were walking along the path of your life, and somewhere halfway you didn't know which direction to take, and you began to think. You came into this life through the front door, but you don't want to leave through the exit. You don't want to leave at all, as you're afraid of the changes that will take place at death. Yet you already went through such a change at birth, and nothing bad happened to you then, only good.

Life, as we know it, is an exercise in the constant improvement of your love. This is not a major quality of life but life itself. For future life to happen, it will be in forms we may not recognize or know.

Happiness

 To be a happy person, know that all the happiness we can want has already been given to us.

Nothing better proves that our major purpose in life is constant improvement than the fact that as soon as you fulfill your desire, you have that desire no longer and you have no joy. The true joy is in understanding that you are constantly moving toward improvement. This constant motion toward self-improvement provides not temporary but lasting joy.

Rejoice! Be joyful! The purpose of life is joy. You should feel joyful for the sky, the sun, the stars, the grass, the trees, the animals, and the people you meet. Be more like children — always be joyful.

If you do what is evil, you yourself suffer. If you do what is good, you thrive and rejoice. You either save or destroy yourself by your actions.

Faith

 True religion is found in one thing — knowing the law that is above all human laws.

There is only one true universal religion — the belief in the one God who is in me and also outside of me, in everyone and every living thing.

The historical attitudes and understanding of God are not more important than the current understanding of God. In the present, God is more and more revealed to us. All past religions should be judged by contemporary forms of religion, not the opposite.

A person changes or perverts religion by thinking that after he makes sacrifices and prays, God will follow his will and serve him. According to true faith, a righteous person knows what God wants him to do — follow His will — and then prays that he can do this, and serve Him.

Soul

 The understanding of yourself — not the physical but your spiritual self — gives you power.

Two things are vital to our life. The first, how we understand our spiritual origin; the second, how this beginning manifests itself in time and space. However, the truth is that only the first exists. The first can be understood but cannot be seen. The second can be seen but cannot be completely understood.

We should not think or say, "I live." We should think and say, "It is not me who lives but the spirit of God living in me."

Opposites attract. It seems to us that life as we know it is made up of what we can physically sense. However, our senses cannot be completely understood, because they do not really exist. What truly exists is our spirit.

One Soul in All

 Everything becomes complicated and confused when we try to pursue our own way in life. When instead of serving our bodily desires, we serve our inner spirit, everything becomes easy and simple.

It is easy to accept your misfortunes when they originate from outer circumstances: illness, fire, earthquakes, and so forth. It is painful for a person to receive misfortunes at the hands of others, those brothers and sisters who should love each other.

If people could understand that they live not only a personal life but through our common life, they would know that when they do good to others they do it to themselves.

People sometimes think that if they were free of God, they would be free. However, the opposite occurs. Those who are truly free are united in God, through His spirit living in us all.

God

 We should not love people but the God in all people.

I began to understand my spirit and started thinking, "What am I?" Just as my body is not really me, my feelings and thoughts are also not me. What is "me," then? I know there is a "me" that nothing could happen without. It is the something inside of me that I call my inner spirit. This is the true "me."

God either does not exist, or exists everywhere, in everything.

Do not be embarrassed that you cannot completely understand God. We cannot describe God with our own words, because this would not be God. However, we can know and feel with certainty that the God we cannot fully understand exists.

Unification in Spirit

 We have only one true guide, our inner spirit that tells us what to do. A tree instinctively moves toward the sun. A flower knows when it is time to make seeds, so its seeds will fall to the ground and grow. Our inner spirits tells us to unite with the spirit that lives everywhere, that speaks to all living creatures.

The world is created in such a way that when ten people are working together, they will produce much more than a hundred people working individually. All our problems do not come from bad harvests, fires, thieves, or enemies, but because we live lives too separate from each other.

The more you love a person, the closer to them you feel. When you love, it seems this person and you are the same.

I will never seek personal salvation. I will always live and strive for the salvation of all.

Universal Love

 We should love people not for their individuality but for the fact that each is our neighbor, who has the spirit of God within. This love will bring us real joy.

In the beginning, the words "love God" seem strange to us. How can we love God when we cannot fully understand Him? When you accept that God is love, these words become simple and clear. To be in love with love itself, to draw close to love, to become a part of love — all this is clear and simple in the heart of every person. We always love God, as He is love itself.

Our body is weak, foul, and subject to death. Yet it has a great treasure inside — the eternal spirit of God. As soon as we understand this, we begin to love everyone, and become happy. — GREGORY SKOVORODA

I was thinking that I was beginning to lose my memory. I forgot I was Leo Tolstoy. What else is left? What is left in me I clearly understand — love, this is what remains.

341

Sin

 The difference between a good and a bad man is not that one is a greater sinner than the other, but that the one knows his sins, tries to get rid of them, and struggles against them, but the other does not know, or care to do so.

If a person says, "It is not worth combating your sins, because no matter how much you fight, you cannot eliminate them," it is the same as if the person said, "Don't give me food, because I'll still be hungry." It is only the struggle against your sins that is the essence of human life.

It is not enough to think you are sinful. You should know in what ways you sin more, and in which you sin less.

Temptation

 If people would eat only when very hungry, and ate only simple, plain food, they would have fewer illnesses, and it would be easy for them to combat other sins and transgressions.

Socrates advised his students to closely monitor which food, drink, and work, and in which amounts, were best for their inner spirit. He said if you did all this carefully, you would be your own best doctor.

Be the boss of your habits; don't let them be the boss of you.

The less we get used to, the less hardship we will endure.

With each passing hour, day, and year more and more people are attracted to vegetarianism. Soon all people will understand the cruelty of killing for the satisfaction of their stomachs.

Desire and Passion

 What should a young man and woman do when the time comes for them to start engaging in sex? The answer is to remain as pure as possible, to choose celibacy if possible. Then your life will be good.

What should a young man and woman do if they get involved in a sexual relationship? They should be married to one another for the rest of their lives.

It was not idly that Jesus praised children so highly and said the kingdom of God belongs to them. What is not revealed to the wise is revealed to children. In every generation and family, we see pure little spirits appear — children who could possibly remain completely pure. Life is like a river filled with mud and dirt, but with many beautiful clean springs flowing into it.

Shame is an expression of a person's natural desire for celibacy. Animals do not feel shame.

Work and Idleness

 The person who does nothing has many assistants.

When the devil went fishing to catch people, he put many different kinds of bait on his hook. However, a lazy person needs no bait. He just swallows a bare hook. The mind of a lazy person is the devil's playground.

One of the biggest misunderstandings we can have is the belief that a person is happy when he is doing nothing — a misconception affirmed in the belief that heaven is the sort of place where people will do nothing.

If a person's daily life is a monotonous routine, he cannot think about his inner, spiritual life. Try to find the spare time to be observant and reflect on your life in solitude.

Greed and Wealth

 People should try to enrich their inner spirit. In reality, most people put their efforts into acquiring as much wealth and as many objects as they can own.

For pagans, wealth is fame and good to achieve; for true Christians, wealth is a sin. To say "a rich Christian" is meaningless, for these words cannot be compared any more than "liquid ice" can.

If wealth is created by deceit such as in trade that separates people or dishonest money-handling or some other temptation, then this wealth, even if some has been given to charity, is much worse than any theft or robbery for which people are punished in a court of law.

No matter how much stuff a person acquires, he will never be satisfied because he will always see others as richer than himself. There is only one way to be happy: be satisfied with what you have and do not wish for more.

After Death

 Everything in this world begins, develops, and ends. This encompasses the fruits of the earth and the seasons of the year. Wise people approaching death see death in the same way.

There is one thing that is important: to know what God wants from us. This is conveyed clearly from without by words, and from within by our conscience, and I understand I must direct all my energy to fulfilling the will of the Master.

The form of our existence disappears, but the inner spirit does not, nor can it, because it exists outside of time and space. It is the only thing that exists.

We can suppose that life after death will start in a way similar to this life — with the understanding of our place in new circumstances.

Happiness

 Asking God to give you something good is just like sitting in front of a spring and asking it to quench your thirst. Good is given to you; you should know how to use it.

There is only one meaning to this life: goodness for all. Life is expressed differently in different creatures so that everyone will rejoice. For humans, good for you is goodness for all.

People often regret what they did not achieve and what they still desire. This matters if you think only of the body, for all that happens is good for the soul. What happens to you is sent by God for your own good.

I think our first rule in this life should be: Always be happy and joyful.